AF486842

A Poetic Memoir

By Joy E. Eshleman

Light Finds Joy: A Poetic Memoir

Copyright © 2026 by Joy E. Eshleman

All rights reserved. No part of this book may be reproduced, distributed, or transmitted in any form or by any means, including photocopying, recording, or other electronic or mechanical methods without the prior written permission of the publisher, except in the case of brief quotations embodied in critical reviews and certain other noncommercial uses permitted by USA copyright law.

Scripture quotations are from The ESV® Bible (The Holy Bible, English Standard Version®), © 2001 by Crossway, a publishing ministry of Good News Publishers. Used by permission. All rights reserved.

Published by Reservoir Books

Contact the author online at http://www.reservoir-resources.com

Printed in the United States of America
First Edition, 2026

Trade Paperback ISBN: 979-8-9950111-0-1

Cover design: Sara Annela Studio

Editing: Rachel Jepsen

To My Creator God
and
the two who named me
and gave me this life,
Mom and Dad

TABLE OF CONTENTS

CHAPTER 4: YOU HAD ME AT CARPET SHOCK

CHAPTER 5: LOVE YOU FOREVER

CHAPTER 6: THE CAREER THAT FOUND ME

ACKNOWLEDGEMENTS

If the ancient African philosophy of communal responsibility were applied to this project, I would say it has taken a village to complete the book you now hold in your hands. My village contains some of the people I hold dearest in my life. From the parents who birthed and raised me to the family I now have, there has been an abundance of influence and care given to me. I am the beneficiary of years of loving relationships and life experiences that have contributed to who I am today.

To the greatest Author of life itself, words barely suffice to thank You for the life you've given me from first to someday last breaths. To my Triune God, I give you deepest devotion and praise.

To my husband, Scott, thank you for being an enduring support and embodying home to me. We have been given an incredible gift of love and marriage through our Lord Jesus.

To my sons, Jonathan and Jesse, thank you for embracing me as your mom and teaching me lessons in life only a child can innocently provide. You are both unique delights and treasured gifts to me.

To my daughters-in-law, Frannie and Lucy, thank you for loving our sons so well and becoming like daughters to me. Both of you joining our family has been the most wonderful surprise and answer to our prayers!

To my granddaughter, Gigi, thank you for your open and trusting heart that has bonded us in the sweetest way. You are the most precious beginning of the third generation of our family.

To my cadre of lifelong friends, the tribe I have been privileged to choose, thank you for being authentically you as we enjoy and share life together. Your encouragement is the bedrock of this book. You know who you are—we've shared many heart to heart moments.

To my editor, Rachel Jepsen, thank you for seeing me and challenging me as a writer as you've embraced my story. Your entrance into my life this past year is something I hold with utmost gratitude.

To my graphic designer and dear friend, Sara Tomeo Aybar, thank you for oozing creativity and providing vision for this project. Your enthusiasm exudes in every aspect of this physical book.

Finally, to you, the reader, thank you for picking up this book. I hope you too find joy.

FOREWORD

Joy was, at the time I met her, a surprising contradiction. I still remember her sternness as she looked over her readers to meet my eyes during an interview. "When did you have the time to write a book?" she asked. I thought, "Uh-oh." All the HR professionals told me not to put that book on the resume—to dumb it down so I wouldn't appear overqualified. So, I buried the things I was most proud of on the back page. Joy noticed. She also noticed months after we began working together the effect of a consultant's unkind behavior towards me even as I fought not to cry in the office. She alerted our Practice Lead and didn't 'flippin' care' who had a problem with it. She cried when she learned I had been having panic attacks since I was 10 or 11. During a months-long workplace crisis she took charge and ran our practice while holding space for what we two were experiencing. Joy can set her face like a flint and do the hard thing, while staying softly usable. She prays. She questions. She processes. She learns. She confronts. Then Joy walks it out.

Joy is the only person who has ever asked me to see "the whole resume" after noticing there were time gaps in the one she held in her hand. This phrase, "the whole resume," became our shorthand for "I'm here for the whole story, not just the parts you're comfortable with or feel good about." Joy and I have navigated highs and lows together, sharing tears, gut-busting laughter, and many cups of coffee. I never expected to call this woman not just a friend, but also a sister. Our relationship is one of my most precious gifts.

The title of this work, *Light Finds Joy*, is a beautiful play on words, because of the author's namesake. Like the contradiction I mentioned above, the posture of joy calls people of faith into its embrace even when things appear hopeless. One of the earliest references in scripture for joy is found in the Old Testament book of Nehemiah. During their weeping and sorrow, God tells his people, "The joy of the Lord is your strength." There is strength in choosing to be joyful, even though joy might stand in stark contrast to what you may be experiencing right now.

Joy writes from the perspective of one who has walked alone and with others through the human experience. Her insights, both spiritual and natural, serve to remind us that our lives don't always happen with peaceful calm waters and sunshiny days. In *Light Finds Joy*, you will experience the childhood giddiness of a first crush, the broken heartedness we go through in the passing of our parents, and everything in between. Our lives can bring happiness and despair the same day. But for those who believe in the finished work of Christ, each experience also provides a chance to find joy in the journey. Imagine how God might show up when we are feeling sorrow because of missed opportunities or feelings of failure. The exploration of our flaws, dysfunctions and fears brought into God's light becomes something of beauty and stands in contradiction to what we perceive as ugly and unacceptable. This is why this work is so unique in its presentation: it's the poetic expression of living that includes how we rise and fall under the watchful eyes of God.

I pray that as you read this book, life's contradictions become the setting for God's light to find you too.

–Michele Aikens

INTRODUCTION

For years I carried this lofty ideal that I would someday write a book. I assumed it would be a chapter book, assuredly non-fiction, imagining that once I began the words would pour out of me onto the page. My first exposure to poetry in grade school, however, awakened something unique and wonderful in me, with its brief invitation to read and then pause to think, digesting its fullness. Chapter books, which were the bulk of primary assigned work, involved a different process, devouring their contents to get to the finale, like satisfaction at the end of a great meal. I found the latter less and less attractive by the time I reached grad school with its voluminous reading rigors. Imagine how freeing it was when I came to terms with the fact that I was never going to write the kind of book I had originally idealized. I wasn't a paragraph and chapter kind of person any longer; I would often read only what piqued my interest and skip the rest.

Writing poetry became a hobby in my teen years and turned into an ally as a college student, literally and literarily. This was the way my thoughts and feelings made it to pen and paper with ease. This was also the way I could summarize an experience without being bothered with grammar rules. Here, teachers weren't correcting my structure and instead were affirming my style and creativity. I also tended to be an adapter of rules, so poetry fit me in a synthesizing way. I love the creative license poetry affords, as it makes room for ideas to flow, perhaps even at times dance, as words lift upwards like a song. At other times it's a painting formed through brushstrokes of thoughts and events, colored by the varying emotions evoked and particularly chosen words to give detail. Simply said, poetry transports me.

It took quite a while for this book to coalesce as a memoir. I had always written for my own sake, to help me process moments and metabolize emotions. It also became a great way to record something I didn't want to forget. In August of 2023 we took two weeks to visit France with our adult sons and daughters-in-law. It was here I began writing about something each day I wanted to remember. Once back to the States I found myself continuing to write daily, often much more than a single poem. Something began to unlock memories and writing prompts inside me—I was surprised at the sheer volume of thoughts and recall that were rolling out of me.

One day while rereading the day's creation, I heard an inner voice suggest that maybe my poems weren't just for me, that they might be for others as well. That was a new thought. Others? Who would find what I was thinking and feeling even the slightest bit relatable? It would still be months before I opened up to a trusted friend about my writing and asked if I could share one of my poems with her. She embodied the perfect blend of excitement and honor in my sharing and set the tone for future readings to others. H.S., I am indebted to you and your extraordinary gift of reception.

Since then, I've shared many poems with friends, family, even clients at times, "sealing" each new complete poem in trust. The notations at the end of pieces throughout this book indicate those with whom I've sealed my poems, something near to my heart with someone I valued.

Writing this book has been a gradual but courageous nudging of my vulnerable self to unashamedly share her soul. I have climbed my way out of my own discomforting thoughts and allowed them to see the light of day. The lesson here is to give them air and let them breathe as a way of lightening our inner burden. We carry too much inside as it is; writing for me is walking out Jesus' invitation to come and trade the heavy pack for his lighter one. The messiness of this process is still holy, even when all that rolls out is far from stunning sunsets and healing hugs. Jesus had no problem with the weight of our struggles; sadly, however, we often lack the trust to bring them to him to receive his promised rest. While hardly anything written here is sermon worthy, remember that was never the goal. Still, the hours collaborating with my Savior have been nothing short of worshipful. For this I am deeply thankful to Him.

I invite you to take your time here, experience my story at different ages and stages, through my eyes, voice, and heart. For me, this is a compassionate recap of my therapeutic journey to integrate life to this point. I've taken intentional time to learn how to embrace my younger self and validate her. For you, I hope you will read a bit and then put it down, an homage to my grade school teacher introducing me to poetry. Let it sit inside you and see what begins to emerge from your own life. It seems we seldom take pause and ponder, especially in our digitally frenzied existence, unless we prioritize this practice. I've found the quiet to be an invitation to listen to my soul and let it speak. Quite unexpectedly, reflection has become a good friend to me. The alternative is missing large swaths of time and insight waiting to be unearthed. If we allow ourselves time to reflect, the discovery ends up being a wonderful archaeological dig with more being revealed the deeper and more patiently we go.

So, can a book of poetry reflect a whole life? My best answer is I believe it's a worthy endeavor. In the pages ahead, I hope you see some of the artifacts of my life and end up with something special emerging for yours.

—Joy

May 8, 2025

CHAPTER 1:

As a little kid, I was determinedly independent, almost as soon as I had memory, and often steadied myself with courage in light of having an older sister. She was my benchmark, the one to beat, having almost three years on me, stronger, bigger, my only competition in our house of two parents and one grandmother, who was my best friend. I had two older half-brothers, 17 and 19 years older, who were already out of the house by the time I knew I had brothers. We moved far too often in my view, rarely living in one place longer than two years. My mom made a point to preface each move with the idea that God had something better for us, otherwise we'd be staying. I didn't realize the effect this statement had on me at the time, but learned that it shaped in me a sense of expectancy for better things. I can recall things from these years in great detail, something I've always been grateful for over the course of my life.

I still remember my first Little Debbie snack cake, the alarm of sitting on an open safety pin, being terrified of *The Wizard of Oz'* flying monkeys, learning to ride a bike on gravel at age nine, and the sound of my little blue toy piano I got for Christmas at age three. I felt sure-footed in the creeks of the Pacific Northwest where we lived from first through fourth grades, stepping confidently from rock to rock, unconcerned about wet shoes. Today I have an aversion to wet clothing and shoes, but younger me actually didn't mind it. My childhood was generally happy, varied with great experiences connected to the different states we lived: Ohio (four places), West Virginia, Alabama, Oregon (four places), and Indiana. My parents were wise to have us vacation in the regions we lived in so that by the time I left for college, I had seen most of the contiguous United States.

I think I was born with a strong sense of justice, wanting things equal and wrongs righted. I began showing my fist at an early age if I didn't like how things were going. My family still sees the show of a lighthearted fist if things don't suit me to this day. Some habits die very slow deaths. In terms of justice, I don't like people being exploited, detest arrogance and self-entitled behaviors, and want everyone to have meaningful things in their lives. If I were to be given a superpower, I would ask to be able to touch any kind of water and make it drinkable for those who thirst. I guess justice takes on different shapes and sizes in me but it does run deep.

PRAISE THE LORD HOUSE

Moved halfway through 1st grade from sunny Alabama
To snowy Oregon in the Pacific Northwest
Where majestic mountains circle the Grand Ronde valley
Like a cereal bowl
It was stunningly beautiful there
Otherworldly

We lived in a named home
On a friend's compound
The Blue Mountain Christian Retreat
With three tiered trout ponds
A babbling creek as one border
Tall white pines lining the lane
Various buildings on the grounds
Ours was Praise the Lord House

My memory bank swiftly flows
Like a tumbling mountain stream
Over and over its frigid rocky bed
Making submerged shins ache
To return to scenes and sounds
That awakened my young senses
I remember them like yesterday

Sound asleep in dreamland
Scooped up and wrapped in robes
Quietly they showed us six deer
Feeding on the snowy yard in winter's moonlight
Like a Christmas postcard
A cherished memory years over

Practicing piano in the old lodge
My sister and I would go there alone
I'll earn a gold star in my piano book
Teaching Little Fingers to Play
Once I can play it perfectly
On the slightly untuned upright
Years later I'm composing my own

If we had other hunts I don't recall
But that Easter it snowed so hard
Eggs were hidden in a foot of snow
I only found them by footprints
Tramped around the yard by my late oldest brother
For us and my toddling niece

Nature was in bounteous supply
Finding giant morel mushrooms with Mama in late spring
She'd discover them first

Then play Hot and Cold with me
Until I'd find them, delightedly,
Bigger than my whole little hand

Grandma showed us how to shell peas and snap green beans
On summer's front porch
We picked Bings and Queen Anne's
Mama canned all of it for winter
While Daddy set a watermelon
In the snow-fed creek before dinner

One standout afternoon
I laid in the soft grass in warm sunlight
By myself
Not a care in the world
Watching cotton clouds waft across
The infinite blue-eyed sky
A gentle breeze kissed my cheek
In this earliest slice of solitude
I was infinitely happy, content, and free

The safety of this remote place
Allowed me to wander and explore
Become sure-footed crossing creeks
Listening for hoot owls and doves
Quietly sitting for long moments
Using Daddy's new binoculars
Sometimes looking at the full moon
Or searching for deer in the woods

I learned to read there
My levels were advanced for only six
My sister and I would play church
Pretending to sing hymns
Until one day it all clicked for me
And I finally got it
Next Sunday's hymns were more fun

We lived there for such a short time
Eight months at most
Before moving across the valley
However brief, it yielded the indelible
Snapshots of colorful moments
Today we call them core memories
Then they were just my little girl life

04 December 23

NAP IN THE CHAIR

Being the youngest of four
I remember it only once
Though it probably happened more

Hugging my mom in the chair
Relaxed, quiet, just us
That kind of time was rare

I remember we sat and talked
Before we both dozed off
My little self wished time could stop

So much demanding her attention
I never got much of her like that
Nap in the chair my grand invention

Think about your younger self
The things you wished
The stuff you missed
Moments being cuddled
Time goes so fast, it's just not fair
What was your nap in the chair?

10 March 25

I CAN DO IT MYSELF

Earliest of memories
Stop smothering me
I don't want your affection
I lean in to her
Arms outstretched
The faked kiss turns
Into a well calculated
I-can-do-it-myself
Bite on her chest instead
This little self hopes now
You'll leave me alone
There's shock and awe
Consequential spank for me
And a future therapy session
For my sister

Standing at the top
Of the wooden stairs
Waiting for Mama
Older sister calls to her
To carry our toys downstairs
Beckons in different voices
Though ineffectual summons
No need to wait
I-can-do-it-myself
Dolls in tow
Descending the stairs
Invincible three-year-old
Scares arriving Mama
Better get used to it

Wading pool
In the front yard
Mama's helping her inside
Don her swimsuit
My turn's next
Confidently I solve the waiting
I-can-do-it-myself
Disrobe right here
Ignore neighbor rebukes
Red hot spanks from Mama
For my impatient choice
No pool time for me
I'd still do it again

Bath time is over
All fresh and ready
For a bedtime snack
Mama brushes sister's hair
Rooms away
Glass 8-pack Pepsi bottles
Sit atop the kitchen stool
I-can-do-it-myself
Almost but not tall enough
Miscalculation brings me
And the carbonated bottles
Crashing to the unforgiving floor
Shards of sticky glass
Shattering everywhere
Even on tiny eyelashes

Determined there's room
In the already full wagon
I-can-do-it-myself
Straddling in tightly
At the very back
Big boy will pull us
His initial labored tug
Yields a jolting hard stop
Sending me backwards
Landing facing the sky
Splitting my four-year-old scalp
Scooped up and bleeding
I'll heal from this cut
It's now a core memory

Perfect time to learn
How to ride that bike
On our paved dead-end street
Mama with surgery stitches
Running far behind me
Intersecting street's traffic
Speeding fast ahead of me
The brakes you tell me
Are on the pedals
But I can't find them
As I pedal furiously
I-can-do-it-myself
Wrecking into a neighbor's grass
Mama nearly splits
Her recovering incisions
Rushing to retrieve me

It's cold outside
We still want to go play
Don't take off your coats—
Do you hear me?
Big sister wants to swing first
I can't push her easily
Wearing this bulky coat
Ethical dilemma for a six-year-old
I-can-do-it-myself
Laying the coat by the tree
Sister is happy, I am free
Until my name hits my ears
Resultant undeserved spank
Future therapy session for me

A sleepover at a friend's house
The eve of my seventh birthday
What fun to wake up
To the big day ahead
Her mom makes us pancakes
Her dad outside with his friend —
Not to her but a stranger to me
Who threatens birthday spanks
I swiftly invent a clever game
I-can-do-it-myself
She innocently follows my lead
So we hide until he leaves
His mean plan is thwarted
By this new seven year old

A birthday party at the park
After school with my friends
I'm nine today and feeling big
It was all so special
Until Mama's coworkers show up
Insisting on nine spanks—each
For this birthday girl
The pained tears result
From stinging smacks gone too far
Mama asks why I'm crying
Gotta save face with my friends
I-can-do-it-myself
Decidedly cover with a lie
"I'm just so happy"

Oh little brown-eyed girl
You were doing the best you could
To solve these moments
The family titled you independent
Maybe it was just cunning
Mixed with self preservation
Weighing and deciding
How to fix things too big for you
With that masterful mantra
I-can-do-it-myself
You still show up inside me
As I make my way to 60

03 November 23

NEIGHBOR GIRL

I'm so little
But I follow my sister around outside
Next door the neighbor girl is her age
We are playmates of convenience
When parents allow

Sometimes we have fun
Sadly can't recall though
Instead it's the not-so-fun tattooed memory
A tent in her side yard
We'll play pretend house
Like little girls do
Until she slaps my sister on her cheek
"Oh I'm sorry"

Resuming our pretend
She slaps her once again
Repeating the sorry
Until sister is crying
Big mad feelings surge in my little body
Now I want to slap the mean neighbor girl

In our teens years
We fuss and fight as sisters do
Escalating to smacks
Snarking out the counterfeit
"Oh I'm sorry" through slit eyes
As if to absolve us
Yet always the winning slap
Leaving the indicting mark
Was calling the other "Chrissy Leonard!"

03 December 23

SEWING BOX

The eight-sided box with fitted lid
Atop three spindled legs
Eighty years old at least
Passed from her mom to my mom to me

When I was four these were my toys:
Wooden spools of thread
Knitting paraphernalia
Red, yellow and blue row counters
Metal bandaid tins of sewing tools —
I have little use for them now
I never learned yarn work
Did I disappoint her?

Her handwritten directions
Of countless little projects
Delicate crocheted chains she tied into yarn bows
Tiny starts of someday big things
Cotton threads of lovely colors
Grandma's buttonhole scissors
With a bag of old buttons
A plastic box of snaps
Salvaged from worn clothes
Unwasted in The Great Depression

Perhaps she'd find
A use for the pill sorter of pearl beads
Or just the right repair moment for safety pins in a jar
I sift through unused ziploc baggies
She surely was saving for something
She saved everything
And a small curl of hair that brings me to tears
It was hers, all of this was hers

I only got to visit its contents
To occupy my little self
When she was needling away
Her kind of grownup play
Her fingers weaving yarns
Needles sewing thread
No longer sitting at her feet
She's here in every piece instead

03 March 25

BILLY

I had paid you no attention
Until kitten day in kindergarten
We were paired to share them
Building them tunnels among the blocks
To walk through in between cuddles

"Hit me."
"What?"
"Hit me."
"I don't want to hit you."
"No, *hit* me!"
"*No*, I'm not going to hit you!"
"HIT ME!"
Distracted with derailing irritation,
Resolute to solve this senseless ask
Kitten in one hand
My other dealt a well-placed slap

Much to my surprise
Instead of satisfaction
Came your dramatic cries
And bellowing distress
All eyes were on me
I was bewildered —
A lightning rod struck within
Splintering my innocence

Disbelief devolved into swift consequence
Escorted to the reading table
To serve a full day's sentence
Privilege now became prison as I hadn't learned to read yet
What did I just do?

Sitting mindlessly turning pages
My fresh glare located its target
With lowered head
My darkened eyes met yours
And your crooked satisfied grin
While holding both kittens

05 October 23
Sealed with MA

BLUE JACKET

It's family night
Load into the station wagon
Drive into town
Eat at Roy's Chuckwagon
See a movie across the street
The mantra before we leave
As per usual, as per always
Bring your sweater
But this time I forgot

Halfway through
Our smorgasbord dinner
The sweater is mentioned
Um, I don't have mine
The theater gets chilly you know
Daddy encourages I hurry up
He walks me to the Five & Dime
And picks out for me
A shiny, tags on, nylon blue jacket

Having an older sister
Means hand-me-downs
Dresses and pant sets
Blue jeans and tops
A little worse for wear
Always worn before me
Our preacher family budget
Could afford these
I don't know otherwise

Here I sit in the dark theater
Wearing my new blue jacket,
The tags proudly still on,
Never worn by anyone before me
Whispering to myself,
"It's all mine" as tiny tears form
It matches next to nothing
And I wear it every day
Never lost or left behind

Maybe in our finite, wanting lives
There's not much to call our own
Nothing new under the sun
But this jacket was my benchmark—
Try to have something real

Something singly all yours
And take such good care of it
For someday it will be passed down
As a used, tags off, blue jacket

RAZING CHICKENS

Fifty little chicks arrived
Cute yellow fuzzy babies
Daddy thought it would be good for us
To learn responsibility
To experience everything involved
In caring for them
I really didn't care
They were just cute

On the third day
They began to transform
From fuzzy to feathery
Tiny signs of ugly emerging
Changing them
Into jerky little demons
The cute was all gone
They were just chores

They grew quickly
The daily feeding and watering
Daddy wanted it done just so
His particularities also emerging
Then eggs began to appear
Often underneath them
In their nests
They were just big

Sister got mumps
So I was left
To tend to the flock
I'd go to the barn
And lob their food
So they'd run away
From me and their eggs
They were just scary

Three weeks was too long
For me to tend them alone
I'd use the broom
To protect myself
I'd stand in the barn
Not feeding or watering
Eggs were diminishing
They were just starving

They protected their nests
Pecking at my flowered coat
Turning their heads sideways
Their beady eyes glaring
Although their enemy
I was terrified every day
Crossing my fingers
They were just dying

Two dead yesterday
Another one today
Daddy joined me in the barn
Show me the way
You've been caring for them
I faked my routine
Until I burst into tears
They were just killing me

Forever in my little mind
They'd be dreaded chores
Some eggs for breakfast
Some eventually butchered
My mantra became
The only good chicken
Is a dead chicken
They were just dinner

He wanted us to learn
To be responsible
Caring for creatures
To this day I actually do both well
What he didn't expect
I'd also learn
Was poultry hatred and murder
They were just extras

07 November 23

For JG

I LIKE A BOY

Blonde feathered hair
Dreamy blue eyes
Great at all sports
Has a killer smile
We're 6th graders
He says, "Let's go together"
I like a boy.

My best friend
Likes his best friend
A perfect dream
We'll probably get married
And live next-door to our best friends
I like a boy with a future.

I watch you glance at me
During our spelling test
You smile and I melt
Dying just a little.

Valentine's Day is coming soon
You arrive at school with a small box
Wrapped in a bow
It's a Speidel bracelet
With my name engraved
On the backside it reads
"From, Alan"
Puppy love feels really big
I like a boy on my wrist.

We last for months
Way longer than grade school romances ever do
My May birthday will be a bowling party with friends
But after Easter you don't smile as much
You don't want to hold my hand
In the field at recess
I watch you talking
To another girl in our class
Then you tell my best friend
To tell me you want to break up
I'm crushed
What about the bracelet?
He says you can keep it
I liked a boy.

02 December 23
Sealed with DaKris

GOD MOMENT

Outpost camp 1977
A bunch of tweenage kids
With a handful of counselors
Sleeping in covered wagons
Eight to be exact
Circling a campfire
One week of roughing it
Cooking our meals outside
Did everything outside really
Until the storm blew in—
"Get to your wagons!"
"Stay inside and nap" were the actual instructions
Seriously?
In this fabric-stretched abode?
Here we were
Four young girls
Scared witless
As the wood and canvas
Rocked and rattled
In torrential rain and winds

It seemed the right thing to do
Hold hands and pray
While the storm pummeled us
It was church camp after all
We sure weren't going to sleep—
As my camp friend mumbled
Her innocent choppy pleas
Somewhere in my mind
I heard Proverbs 3:24
No idea why or what this was
So I pushed it away
Again somewhere Proverbs 3:24
Rejoin the asks and ignore more
Again stronger Proverbs 3:24
Finally opened my kid Bible
And found its page
While my wagon mates
Kept praying, eyes tightly shut

When you lie down
You will not be afraid
When you lie down
Your sleep will be sweet
Do not fear sudden danger—
I was stunned to read this

What was this?
How did it fit so well?
Where did this come from?
What part of my young brain
Had this in safe keeping
For this one storm-filled moment?

If He was, He was right then
My mind darting
Back and forth
Rereading the words
This did not come from me
I'd never read it before
He was real
He had to be real
For He delivered a secret
To my wanting heart
I was forever changed
This the first of many
This my first God moment

19 December 23

CHILDHOOD FRIENDS

Presbyterian kindergarten
New transplant to Alabama
Three moves by age five
Cookie was my friend
Her real name escapes me
I especially loved the party
For her half birthday
Cake on half paper plates, so fun

Two moves in to Oregon
Shaunda was my red hair, freckled friend
Who lived down the long lane
We'd meet halfway sending birdcalls
My only pal for sleepovers, sledding and pancakes
The other potential friend nearby
Was three standard deviations from cool so, no

Ohio in sixth grade
Kami was my friend
A perfect penmanship gymnast
Bonds of passing notes and inside jokes
Best friends who liked best friends
I finally found my person
Sad was the day I moved away
Instead letters into high school

I'm sure there were others
But these were the three
My memory treasures
The only wrinkle in finding them
Girls' last names change
Unlike boys
My moves prompted eventual ends
Still I loved my childhood friends

04 August 24

WHAT ABOUT OUR LITTLE GIRLS?

It's not an easy life
For little girls
With a restless daddy
Working out his own stuff.

I was born in St. Mary's Ohio 1964
Move #1 was to Waterville as a baby
Until Daddy was fired in 1967
For walking the D.C. Peace March
The church couldn't align
With his convictions.

Move #2 at age three
To Parkersburg West Virginia
I can still taste the grape gumballs
From the store
At the bottom of the hill
Never found any better
And boy have I searched them out
Like forever.

Age five we're off again move #3
Right before kindergarten
This time Tuscaloosa Alabama
Where we are the minority now
The only white family
In a deeply loving
All black church
On the Stillman College campus.

Age six and a half we're heading west
To LaGrande Oregon move #4
At the halfway point of first grade
Where I met my favorite teacher
And she helped me settle in
So much to settle into
For such a little girl
Teach her to read – quickly
Before she has move #5
Eight months later.

We'd have moves #6 #7 #8
In the Grand Ronde Valley
Over four short years
Each requiring a school change
Always the new kids
Friendships so short lived
Did he ever stop and ask
What about our little girls?

A painful family letter arrived
Asking for a visit back in Ohio
A cry for help actually
Turned into move #9
Starting fifth grade
Living at my oldest brother's home
While Mom and Dad went back
To pack up life in Oregon.

Continued fifth grade
When Mom and Dad returned
Six weeks later and settled us
In a nearby community
Move #10 to yet another school
Liking boys in every class
A pro at identifying the mean girls
And the kids who teased me
About my ears and my nose
In every school
The new kid is always a target
Who does this to little girls?

I'd make a best friend here
At Luckey Elementary School
So the impending 11th move
Made this one hardest for me
I'd be starting seventh grade
In a new state
In a new small town
Moving was getting so old
I just wanted to stay here
Can we please just stay here?

Eleven moves
Five states
A full circle
Around the country
I was definitely in a state
Arriving in junior high
Didn't want to be here
In Indiana of all places
Conditioned to land
Only temporarily
Don't get too attached
To anyone or anything
How sad.

Did they lay in bed at night
Considering us?
Wonder how all the chaotic change
Would affect and shape us?
Impact how we'd ever attach
To anyone longer than two years?
They are long gone now
So I'll never get to ask

09 December 23

CHAPTER 2:

Being a pastor's kid was rough. I didn't like the moniker or the unfair assumptions that came with it. Starting seventh grade in a new small town was the worst possible setup to discover people were curiously sizing up this novel pastor's family. I felt eyes on me walking to our main street's Rexall Drugs, at the freezing fall football games, and of course at church. While I was too young to be a hellion just yet, I swiftly worked to nullify any notion I was a goody-two-shoes target for teasing. No one coached me how to live two separate lives; while it seemed to be working on the outside, my internal world was disintegrating. Incongruence at any age isn't sustainable unless we master lying to ourselves. Daily I was homesick for my best friend in Ohio, alongside the guilt of juggling being two different people with my peers versus anyone connected to the church. While I didn't know the term double life, I was living as such just to cope with this tumultuous time in my life.

I made friends every time we relocated, 11 times by seventh grade, mostly as a means of survival, but sometimes because they were people I genuinely liked. I got a high school job before any of my friends, often spotting for gas, food, and anything else that fueled my thrill to be the girl in charge. In our small town high school I relished the dream (and still do) of someday being conversant in French, making it through to college towards the top of my class as I excelled in most subjects except math. My penmanship was categorically some of the worst with a few professors asking me to type my homework, reaffirming my being the last inductee into the 6th grade handwriting club. While my scribbles might have been one more way to keep people at bay in those awkward years, I am indebted to my 6th grade teacher, Mrs. Snyder, who cleverly motivated me to improve.

In those teen years, I tried on a lot of boys for size, none of them sufficing to match the depths of my interests nor my feistiness and fire. And as it so often goes, the ones I wanted didn't want me. Instead they confessed they treasured me as a friend, the golden friend you'd never want to lose. They intimated they wouldn't want romance to ruin that kind of friendship. Sounded almost noble, but still felt like a cop-out excuse. Here's to all you boys I thought I loved! While the wish for a steady boyfriend never materialized, having one at that age would've most likely landed me in trouble, so God was wise to not deliver on that wish. Somehow I still managed to attend four proms, though always "just as friends." I've turned out pretty decently without the high school boyfriend, so take heart if this was your wish too.

PAST

If you brought my past
Out for a visit
I'd say I knew that girl
And I felt for her

I'd say she was a mixture
Of guts and confidence
Longings and rejections
Stupidity and fool's gold

She needed support
But supported others
Instead
Off everyone's radar

She'd sit on her bed
Staring out the window
Losing hours
Undetectably depressed

Good grades
Clever wit
Daring risks
People radar

Preoccupied parents
Smile for the camera
Live a double life
No one knew

She couldn't sustain it
And broke
Just let me die
In my sleep

I see her now
All grown up
I've helped her heal
And become me

08 September 21

ANONYMOUS

New town
Small town
Way too small
For this new girl

Starting junior high
Too many times
Someone would rattle off
Who I was
Like they knew me

Just because
My dad was the new pastor
Of the Presbyterian Church
Just because
We were the novelties
In this tiny town

Worst thing you can do
For a young school girl
Is detail her particulars
As if she didn't know
Her name
Her grade
Her dad's job
Her sister's grade
Her being new in town

Please stop talking
And let me shapeshift
Under the table
And ooze away
Unnoticed
Better yet
Let me blink you away
With my eyes like a wand

Maybe it's your way
Of being friendly
But to me
It's off-putting and jarring
I don't know you

So how do you know
All this stuff about me
Unless I was gossip fodder
At the Rexall soda counter
More bothersome yet
You don't ever try
To get to know me

Familiarity isn't friendship
I'd rather fly
Under your radar
Anonymous

02 Dec 23

TRAPPED

I was newly twelve
I didn't want this—
Another move
Another state
Leaving my best friend
My first real best friend
Someone so hard to find
When you move so often

My station in life
Preceded me
Small town busybodies
Broadcasting our arrival
The new pastor's family
I'm going into seventh
The most awkward stage
To stand out

I didn't take well to notoriety
My peers singled me out
Naming me Miss Holy
It was gaining traction
More than I imagined
I hated it —
But there was an image to maintain
Even for a 12-year-old
Because of my dad

I made a few friends
None like the one I left behind
But enough to survive
If only I could blend in
My decided strategy
To follow their examples
Live two dissonant lives
One at church, one at school
One routinizing faith
One projecting cool

Shortsighted plan didn't deliver
I pressed in harder
Dropping curses and f-bombs
I'll be anything
But Miss Holy
Then they'll leave me alone
They have to leave me alone
Please just leave me alone
I'm so miserably alone

No surprise what came to pass
Lava on the inside
Cool on the outside
Facade of togetherness
Everything looked good
But what a lie
You reap what you sow

I didn't ask for that life
People faked they knew me
Depressed kid undetected
Just play the game
So shame infected
Counting the days
Until it was all in the rearview
Metaphoric tires peeling out

How does one so young
Become so enclosed
Socially straightjacketed
Before she's even begun to blossom and bloom
It took years to find the exit
Never looking back
Finding a freer life
No longer trapped

14 May 24

SPELLING BEE

English class seventh grade
I was the new girl
One semester earlier
We learned the rhyme
Of helping verbs
And spelling big words
I was good
Really quite good
Each of us got a chance
To advance
But one by one disqualified
By misspellings and errors
I made it to the finals—
Teacher's version
Of a spelling bee

Something strange
Began to happen
Round after matched round
The ones I thought
Were my friends
Starting cheering
For my opponent
Remember this—
I'm on my own now—
And that damn word
That I can't spell
To this day
"OCCURRED"
Ending my run
Sealing my ruin

Afterwards
I walked down the hall
To the lunchroom
And still sat with them
Those who cheered on
The nerdy winner
The one they'll never include
At the lunch table
No less invite into their circle
They adeptly disqualify
Anyone who's different
Smarter, better
But my true friends?
Well I won't meet mine
For another twenty years

08 November 23
Sealed with L.L.E.

PAST STUFF

I'm never going to go there
Yet in my mind
I still walk it back
I still set these memories
Out on the paint chipped
Picnic table
To get some sun
To bake just a bit more
The overlay of varnish peeling
Into iridescent curls
Kind of pretty
Kind of sad
Actually more than kind of

Maybe it's more beautiful
As is
The now idealizing
What was
I still see you
Brown tousled curls
Eyes dancing with life
A smile meant just for me
Catches me blushing
Emotions turning and twirling
Invisible to all but you
You know it as well as I do
We won't get this back

Sweep me up into arms
Strong and moving
While holding me still
Feet lifting off the ground
To something far more sure
Measured in nanoseconds at best
Before returning to earth
With gravity pulling against its flight
Nothing lasts forever
If it did
There'd be no reason for recall
No finger retracing
Past stuff

19 April 24

FIRST LOVE

I was 16 going on 21
Your age and me wishing I was
Your eyes danced with mischief
When you'd smile
And I was so readily smitten
As were you
Our infrequent visits were so bright
In between dark spans of time
I missed you terribly
My heart would actually ache
To see you, hear your voice
Feel your hugging arms
Your letters felt like whispers
That would hold me close
Until breath on my cheek
And soft heartbeats once again

We were such a great pair
Volleying wit and humor
Lots of faith talks
Showing me verses you loved
Deep moments for being so young
Trouble of the best kind
And oh you were so kind
Those "love you's" were life for me
I thought time between our visits
Would end me
But you had me
Sweetly wrapped
In your all-consuming hold

Your last visit promised
Something you wanted to tell me
I was nearly overwhelmed with hope
Would this be it, finally,
We make it forever?
We stayed up all night
Your words fell into tender soil
I can't believe what you're saying
You're engaged
To another
Her dad offered you a job
Everything was crumbling
Falling into my breaking heart

You tried to console
But I wanted to die
Did I misunderstand?
How did I get this so utterly wrong?

You said I was young
With a bright future waiting for me
How in the world without you,
Without us?
I forced myself upstairs to bed
But I did not sleep
For days
And elongated nights
I was destroyed—
Once I could sleep
I prayed I wouldn't wake up
Completely inconsolable
No one knew how to help

I couldn't sustain this pain
Stomach sick from days of tears
Mom mentioned a verse
That gripped my mind until I could find it
Upstairs in my room I knelt
Challenging God Himself
If you're real, show me
No windows were open
But a draft caught my breath
Stopping my tears, instantly scared
Now what?
God?

So I knelt each night for weeks
Terrified this comfort would vanish
Being left alone more than before
As I clung to this God-anchor
Something began to shift over time
Though my heart took years
Your God-bottle caught my tears
I poured through the good book
Scouring for comfort
Like a beggar for food
Come to me all who are weary
Heavy burdened
Faith began to grow
Where love was left as dust
And then, surprisingly, came trust
It is better to trust in God
Than to trust in kings and princes

The years have grown me
I see things differently
While he left me so young
And chose life with another
I was also left an important gift
That I would need more
Than I needed him

It took years to unwrap
And heal
I am indebted to heartbreak
For teaching me true pain
And eventually strength
Sweetly introducing me
To my First Love

05 November 23

CHAPTER 3:

Leaving for college was on the heels of losing my best friend, my maternal grandmother, one month beforehand. She was the one I told my secrets and made up stories, the best back scratcher and afternoon nap buddy. She taught me card games, how to scramble eggs, basic yarn work, snapping beans and shelling peas, whatever she taught, I was her little sponge. Her death hit me like no other loss to that point in my life and I ended up starting college with mononucleosis. While it may fondly be known as the "kissing disease," I'm sad to say that my grief was the vehicle that served to flatline my immune system. So here I was, entering a completely foreign life phase with mono and without her. My parents unloaded my stuff into my room and left almost immediately for my dad to get back to conduct a wedding. There was no run to Target for unexpected items, no final nice dinner out, just some hugs and "call us Sunday night." The first 24 hours felt like an out of body experience for me, alone and unsure how to set up my room since my roommate was arriving two days later. Somehow I figured it out, independence kicking in to survive the unfamiliar yet again.

Because I graduated fourth in my high school class, I felt overly confident academically only to jarringly discover my small-town education hadn't equipped me with reliable study skills. I landed my first mid-term "D" a few weeks into that first semester. This was a jolt to my ego, realizing I was surrounded by people who had the same accolades or better. We were all super achievers, which meant starting over at the same place as everyone else and having to find my way near the top over a series of semesters.

Making new friends came quickly and easily, an acquired skill from all those childhood moves. I discovered through the first semester, however, that your first friends won't be your last friends. Serendipitously, I bonded with my roommate, who also had mono. We roomed together three years, experiencing notable strain after we added additional roommates to the mix. On graduation day, we shared a meaningful moment of eye contact after very few interactions that senior year. She in that moment served as the bookends to my college experience, which felt like some sort of kind and needful closure.

I found myself transitioning from being the independent one in my family to now truly having to depend on myself. I had wanted this new-found freedom for so long that I took full advantage of it, making some pretty poor choices from the start and then having to climb my way back to sanity and stability my second semester and beyond. Finally I was surrounded with college all-stars I found interesting; this pool of young men to befriend was like a candy store to me, some were good and others just plenty. In terms of dating however, no guy grabbed my attention for more than a date or two, after a freshman train-wreck relationship. I had two very close male friends who were the only I'd even consider pursuing a serious relationship with but both were either dating someone else or hesitant to change our friendship into something more and risk losing it altogether. I watched my other college roommates parade a series of mixed relationships in front of me and decided if what they had was love, I didn't want it. At some point in my senior year, I decided instead that I would adopt and be a single mom rather than have relationships like those. While part of that idea worked for me, the backside was I would've loved to have someone be mine, even if soon after it crashed and burned.

Those four years were such a wonderful time in my life. I loved being stretched out of my comfort zone in many ways and embraced critical thinking like no time before, something I treasure to this day in my work as a counselor. Faith that I would call my own grew and was lived out in the tension of being an Inter-Varsity Christian Fellowship President alongside being a little sister in a fraternity. Somehow these two worlds eventually found a way to be integrated over many failed attempts and restarts. I embraced being a leader in many campus organizations and glided on my accolades straight to graduation. Identity was nicely formed here and served as a sturdy launching pad for the next tasks of young adulthood. By then I had learned how to "dress for success", navigate a vast array of relationships, lean into my faith, and operate with decent self-awareness as I moved beyond college.

I fondly recall professors who made deep impressions on me both in my degree coursework and in the elective classes I chose. One that stands out as I pen this book is my creative writing professor who challenged me to dig deep and write whatever surfaced. Thank you, Dr. Guillory, wherever you are, for seeing something in me and encouraging its growth.

NO IDEA WHAT I'M DOING

Headed off to college
Outwardly self-assured
Yet no idea what I was doing
Barely a penny to my name
After making the big purchase
But oh how I loved
My electronic correcting typewriter

It was a beloved four years—
Small enough school
Where everybody knew my name
I embraced all the extracurriculars
While too independent for a sorority
Somehow found my belonging
As frat Little Sister of the Year, *twice*

Late night ramen in hot pots
Popcorn poppers at any hour
We dragged ourselves to 8am's
Fall football and homecomings
Clique-ish tables in the "caf"
My dad was even an alumnus
But I made it my school

It was the 80's era of big hair
Dance parties and drinking shoes
Blowing off class for a nap
Breaking my first bone - my nose
Resembling a bruised hockey player
My friends took great care of me
I wouldn't change it for anything

The headaches, the heartbreaks
President of this and that
Committee lead of such and so
How I hated to let it go
But out beyond to graduated pasture
Life was coming at me ever faster
Still no idea what I was doing

13 August 25

CEDAR CAMPUS

It was chilly
For May
After a full day
Of learning
Leaning in
Listening

Too early
For goodnight
So we made our way
To a picnic table
By the dock
Let's stay up

Future college grads
Talking till predawn
Our back and forth
Perfect really
The night sky
Dancing with color

I don't recall
Which was greater
Your company
Or the northern lights
First time in view—
I'm pretty sure it was you

07 January 24

FRIDAY 1:15 PM

Can't concentrate in class today
Have no intentions
Of paying attention
Classroom in decay
Register spewing
Professor talking at class
No response elicited

Preoccupation is a simple yet great joy
Allowing me to escape this drab environment
Playing with thoughts that no one suspects
Faces dead of expression
Indicative of being uninterested

"Wherever you are, be all there."
So often advised
Rarely implemented
Remaining a deadwood phrase
All do their own thing
Regardless of what's suggested
All have their own thoughts
As the lecture drones on

11 October 84

SECRET MOMENT

The look that rests upon your face
Words unspoken find a place
Within your heart and nestle there-
A gentle smile is all you share

Was this the first time that you blushed?
You words have never been so hushed
This unvoiced thought bids you remain
Mute, as silence finds its gain

And as I gaze into your eyes
This quietude has made me wise—
Some things are better left unsaid:
Without this, longing would be dead

31 January 86

DEATH OF PERFECTION

It was too much
Pressurized
Stress

My inner critic was
Intensely
Weary

All the fun was
Choked
Out

No longer able
To sustain
Striving

It was my decision
To end the precision
It was time

Freedom came
In approximations
Estimations

No longer bound
But guided by
Gentler reductions

13 September 22

1982

It could've been worse
Yet so bad in undoing me
Newly graduated
Near the top of my class
That summer turned dark
When she left us, she left me
I was suddenly alone
No one knew me like her
All I'd held on to
Went with her final breaths
I didn't even get to say goodbye

I left for college in pieces
Left my grieving parents too
I waffled and wandered
Through new places, new faces
Unable to deny how adrift I was now
This my first encounter with death
She my anchor all those years
The chain now broken
Left me to hide behind coolness
Swallowing invisible tears
In a new place without her

Overlaying my heart
With other lesser things
All the parties and boys
As if they could fill the void
Still grief ate at me, drained me
Dead inside but looking alive
No one knew me here
I wouldn't let them know my loss
I'll find a way to get by
Collapsing into chaos
Dreams gone sideways
Poetry became my vice
Among other things tried on for size
Foolishly gave myself away
Though nothing left to take
I'd see glimpses of her glittery gray
Sometimes in an aging professor
All the while a walking, partial heart
Losing your best friend doesn't heal well

27 August 23
For Grandma

LEAVE ME WHERE I LEFT YOU

At first it was mutual
Inside jokes and banter
The skips of acquainting
With somebody new

The calls at odd times
The cards left in my mailbox
Comparing schedules
Attempting meetups
Until we did

Lots of sleep lost
For just a few more minutes
That became hours
The walk back to the dorm
Slow, draggingly tired

The shortest romance
Ruined by other girls
Who catch your eye
I won't be the fool ever
So I call it and walk away
You find that unbelievable

Yet you persist with charm
While tempting, my pride wins out
You send messengers
In hopes I'll cave in
I don't and you won't relent

You fail out freshman year
After baseball season
The best friend from your town
Now your pony express
I hold my ground with No

The week before my graduation
Yet one more final plea
You want to see me, while true
It would have never worked
It's time to leave me where I left you

18 May 24

WELCOME TO HELL

All twenty-three years of me
Felt jarringly like fourteen
As soon as I stepped out
On the factory floor
Me the newly appointed babysitter
To the graveyard shift's crew
Two nights earlier some cretin
Dropped a cereal toy figurine
Into the hot glue vat as a joke
Shutting down the line
Giving everyone a day of hooky
While glue pipes were repaired

Their punishment was second shift—
Mine was having a college degree
Thus qualifying me to supervise
Or more accurately be subjected to
Them—
Twelve high seniority union misfits
Who ruled the third shift with fists
Hated everyone in the front office
The cowards who sent me
To fill the temporary assignment
Instead of sending one of their own

"Welcome to Hell!!" rose above
The manufacturing noise
His dark eyes meeting mine
Accompanied with a vile grin
His plan to intimidate
Turned my summer blood cold
Someone in earshot touted
"This is gonna be fun"
All eyes on me
And my useless supervisor clipboard
No college degree could change
The air in the room choking my breath

So began the three-week assignment
Of 3–to–11's
Missing my friends
My day–shift front–office job
My comfort zone in cocky town
Instead, twelve out to break me
Find my weaknesses
Laugh at my untimely end
Like wolves licking their chops
Before devouring their prey

I'm not going to make it
I can't do this I told my boyfriend
They are hateful and cruel
Scaring the crap out of me
Making sport of me
Their well-protected ego fortresses
Barricaded off as if not human
Difficult, unruly, uncooperative fronts
Shielding their real selves
But somehow I could see them

Determined not to be a meal
Shift by shift I sat beside each one
Swallowing my impending doom
Pushing myself to ask their stories
Listening to those willing to share
Learning they were men
With hearts and families
Divorces and child support
Bills to pay and union dues
Tired of being treated second–class
For most of their hard-luck lives
By men in the front office of society

The fourth night of the second week
Mr. Welcome to Hell
Protectively walked me to my car
Not all of us are good guys
You don't deserve our abuse
I've got your back
Be safe driving home—
My summer blood began to thaw

One of the hardest of the crew
Came to my glass windowed office the next day
You're still here?
We haven't finished you off yet?
An hour of honest talk revealed
He the most vulnerable of the gang
Curious how I kept returning
Night after night
Taking their shit without buckling
I couldn't do this if I was you

By next week's end relief arrived
Strangely bittersweet it was over
I filed my reports, said my goodbyes
Waved them off one by one
Name by name, man by man
Each having taught me something

I didn't know I lacked or needed
Each proving everyone is worth
Something, someway
If you only genuinely accept
Their welcome to Hell

18 December 24
Sealed with DSE, J&I.

CHAPTER 4:

Post college, I tried out a serious relationship that ended in disaster by my choosing. Never date anyone out of pity. Please re-read that last sentence. Once I admitted to myself that I was dating him out of something other than love, I had to end it. Much to my surprise was the one who arrived shortly after, who came into the room like a tornado and accessed parts of my heart that none had before. I fell in love with him, poetic prose pouring out of me page after page. We were long-distance for 15 months after starting our dating in the same city and church for six months. He took his first job after grad school in Florida while I headed to grad school in the Chicago area. We got engaged halfway through our time apart. Back then, phone calls were long distance over a land line and the rates varied depending on what day and what time of day we called. So we wrote letters often and visited in person less often on my school breaks. Two weeks into being married I felt the drop in my mood, having been conditioned by our long distance hellos and goodbyes. At that moment I had this epiphany that we didn't have to say goodbye ever again. This is to date one of the best moments of my life.

We are still married, approaching nearly 40 years now, and believe me, he is a good man as I am no picnic to live with. I gave him a book filled with pages of love on our wedding day, thinking this would be a treasure to him for years to come. Just recently I learned he didn't actually read it until years later, discovering, but not remembering, it was a wedding gift. Some things like this get lost in the midst of living and so it was with the gifted book. It eventually matured in value.

Love and marriage often go that way, especially when both lose some of their shine over time. I knew being together would have both its treasures and its tolls. Naïveté would swear that's untrue but réalité confirms otherwise. Always make room for that in the halls of love. There was an elongated season of marital pain that we openly share with others, attesting to faith as our anchor. Marriage really isn't about two people, as much as we try to convince ourselves of this. The Author of marriage needs to be central for anything good to come from it. Staying close to Jesus saved us, the only words I remember promising in our vows in 1989.

I've come to the realization that he is my home much more so than the roof above our heads. I think it's lovely to find your home in a person rather than an address. To echo Will Thacker's pitied friend's words in the film *Notting Hill*, the fact that anyone ends up with a lifelong love is pretty remarkable in this world. This finds me thankful and humbled to this day.

DECEMBER

december
the snow came
and the whiteness began
to cover cold ground
the wind blew
not to chill
but to remind us
we need warmth
i found an ember in the snow—
i held it in my hand for a short time
and i was warm

without fuel
and protection from the wind
the ember would die
i placed this ember in a large fire
where it could glow
so as not to smother it in my glove
the ember stays alive longer in the fire
than if i let it smolder
in my palm

i would rather keep warm
before God's hearth
especially while it is near
its radiant glow is pure—
it refines all that embrace it
without this flame
there can be no fire
stay close and we will know
God's warmth

december
the snow came
and we were warm

1 December 87

ROMANTIC PANIC

This overwhelming sentiment
Wells up and rolls out of me
Like a gala red carpet
Only two in attendance
Such moonstruck insanity
Where did this come from…
You show up on the inside of me
And everything rearranges

Once I voice it
It becomes real and true
All my terror in the room
Even if for a fleeting second
This isn't like me
I've scoffed at glazed eyes
I don't recognize myself
Until I look into yours

Can you take my hand
And calm me
Lead me around and show me
What's familiar
Things I only recognize
When you're near
Then I'll settle into your side
Safe, warm, nothing to hide

29 August 23

P.S.

I love postscripts
More than most scripts
Words penned in ink
What you feel and think
Sweetest of afterthoughts
Between you and me
They're just for me—
I'd most likely
Love you forever
Simply based on
Your treasured final words
Like an ending note
Of the song you just wrote
Landing on my heart
Like chords from keys

I glory in inking
All that I'm thinking
And endlessly feeling
Such hope and love
But then there's just one more
Closing thought that unfolds
Something like this
P.S.
Just making sure
You now have
The sum of all of them
Every last one of them
I'll hold nothing back from you—

Sweet postscript
Wanting you to know
You're my last thought
You're my best thought
And always will be
Whatever comes next
Will make its way
Into a new penned letter
And I promise
There will always be
A P.S.
From me

P.S. I had hoped to dream of you last night. I thought about you so long I
believe I never slept. While we're apart, I relish more nights like this my love.
Yes, please, if we must be apart.

11 Dec 23

I LIKE YOU HERE

I like
Sitting across the table
From you

I like
Your voice
In my ear

I like
Watching you smile
With your eyes

I like
Your laugh that steals
My heart

I like
Your strong hands
Holding mine

I like
Truly
Having you here

02 January 24

MATCH

If there had been a marriage
There would've also been a divorce
This first one was not my match
Discovering his moods
Led to hard, pointed questions—
The deciding one:
Do you ever think of us
Not together?
Quickly he replied,
"I don't want to be alone"
The absolute worst wrong answer
Hit my heart like a fist
So I ended it
Because I'm too damn special
To just be a warm body
I hear he found another one
Six months later

This second one was so different
Socked feet shuffling across carpet
Touching an electric spark
To my nose
My sister laughed
And said you were perfect
Opposites attract but
Likenesses keep you together
Fifteen inches between us
I said I'd never
Marry someone tall
What is said about saying never?

Even the best of marriages
Take a lot of hard work
It's more about fixing what breaks
Than coffee and wedding cake
Words tumble out of my mouth
Sometimes on purpose—
Making such a mess
So I get out the apology mop
My pride dragging it slowly
And start cleaning it up

You have your ways too
Quieter than mine
You say less, a lot less
But your heart is kind
You are loving and loyal
My home
My front-pocket person

God-fearing
Helpful to others
Without motives or ego
Your clever wit brings laughter
There's so much laughter

Your attention to detail
My big picture view
You support my growth
Without fear I'll eclipse you
You're the hardest worker
Unstoppable at times
I strive for work/life balance
But don't hit as hard as you
Your consistency dances circles
Around my starts and stops
You are warmth
Even when your hands are cold

We are road trip masters
Loving our adventures for two
Standing amid saguaro cacti
Your turn to me delighted
And say, "Thank you for this!"
You're such a great sport
For my many ideas in motion
And you hike, man can you hike
Alone, because it's not my thing
And you're okay with that
Because I prefer beach glass hunts
And we reunite fulfilled
Better for it
Better now together again

Who knew that carpet shock
Would ignite a flame for life?
God did and I do too
Because you are my match

05 November 23

WORK TRIP

Packed bag of pressed shirts
Cup of coffee
Kiss goodbye
Alone

Another wave from the driveway
Another work trip
Another day
Gone

Greet hello in the driveway
Big hug
Another day
Together

Unpacked bag of wrinkled shirts
Cup of coffee
Kiss goodnight
Home

06 April 87

WHITEWATER

When things are headed south
Thoughts can go
Farther south
Into places we've never gone before
Veering off course
Of course
To the desperate outer reaches
Reaching for anything
To keep us from drowning
To keep it all from dying

———————

We started off rafting
Class 2 whitewater, a 3 at most
Assuredly bumpy
Yet doable and fun
Sun high in the sky
Ever so slowly, unnoticeably
Adventure turning dark
Momentum is building
As we move farther downstream
Like it's now the guide
Whether I want it to
Lead me or be in charge
Rapid water tumbles
Rotating and turning
In on itself
Debris floating by
Damage is growing
Everywhere I look
Huge trees become toothpicks
Swept into this raging flow
I can only watch it happen
As I'm dragged into its path

Our raft gave way
Farther upstream
We're grasping for outcroppings
Of roots in embankments
None strong that can save us
I'm completely alone now
No idea where you are
Rapids rage with vengeance
Either be impaled on the rocks
Or snagged by splintered branches
Won't make it out alive
Without a miracle
GOD HELP ME
All other words fail me

I'm carried with bruises
Now painting my flesh
Blood visible amid cuts
From deluges
Of sticks and stones

I can barely see ahead
A white jacket is dangling
From an overhead branch
Like its waiting to rescue
And I'm nearly dead
Steer myself in its direction
With all I've got left
It's all I've got left
To grab and hold onto
For life dearer than this
Please lift me from this

Somehow I'm planted
On a higher embankment
Don't know how I got here
But I'm out of the torrents
At least for the moment
Assess all the damage
It's bad but not ruined
I guess I'm not ruined

Sit like an immoveable boulder
Clinging to ground beneath me
The only thing solid
For the first time
In a long time
Gather my senses
I think I'll survive this
What was it that got me
Out of destruction
And back on dry ground
As I drip dry and cry

You cried out the same
GOD HELP ME
As I did
Somehow you made it
To the other side
Battered and broken
Pulling yourself out
Of the deadly course
With breathy prayers

I can barely see you
The waters divide us
A gaping carved chasm
Will take all our strength left
To cross shaking with terror
Or meet somewhere downstream
Where it's safer and calmer
I can't even imagine
How we will end up there
But I'll meet you there
Catching glimpses of you
Struggling to walk the other bank
Each step a bit stronger
Than the one before
Was this just a pained metaphor
For our nearly failed marriage

06 December 23

60 GOING ON 22

Let's ride together a little bit longer
Drink the coffee now so much stronger
Not fully sure how I ended up here
But the sky is finally a much clearer blue
There's nothing else for me but to smile
I'm 60 going on 22, back to when we met

We've come so far, decades really
Miles of good years
Some with painful tears
Through lots of fights
Troubled nights
To where we are now

I wouldn't have believed it myself
But hard work hanging on
While we were hanging out
Made those doubts disappear
Never packed to travel through hell
Never dreamed it could turn out this well

Now I see the cloudless expanse
When I look into your blue eyes
It's taken us years
To become who we are
I think we are finally
Free of disguise

03 May 23

MINUS 8

It's minus 8 outside
The furnace hasn't slept
Coffee and a snoozing dog
For company
You left for the airport
Middle of the night
Couldn't go back to sleep
Instead I'm up before dawn

These trips aren't so bad
When I have songbirds
Announcing the day
But dead of winter
Has taken them south
Where you're headed
Ice and bitter cold
Cannot sing to me

I lean into the day
Reluctantly
Quietly
No appointments
Nowhere to be
On this subzero Monday
The clock will sleep too
While I singly miss you

15 January 24

US

You love solitude
I love people
You bike and run
While I enjoy the sun
You're meat and potatoes
I'm coffee and cake
Mennonite
Presbyterian
Oldest
Youngest
But God
Between us

You asked me
To marry you
Minutes into
Christmas
At a construction site
That you recall
Was at a lake
At midnight
Apparently I paused
Nerve rackingly long
But I said yes
To all of you
Ring size unknown
Somehow fit perfectly
Like us

We've moved
From the opposites
Closer to the middle
Finding the good
In each others' ways
Learning the better
Over thousands of days
Your misspellings
And things similar to words
Always catch me
Laughter rolls out
Cutting in line ahead of
Translating
Anticipating
Your next try
To clarify
I smile

You're truly so great
Please don't change
Don't become
A better speller
You are my burst of joy

CHAPTER 5:

Two amazing sons came along in our early thirties and I say to this day I've loved every age and stage of having kids. They are the greatest accomplishment in my lifetime and the deepest delight of this mother's heart. I've said for years that each child teaches you something as a parent you needed but wouldn't learn otherwise without such intense exposure. One taught me flexibility to bend and adapt when things dramatically change in a split second, forcing you to punt with no foreknowledge of what's coming. The other taught me patience, the kind that stays in the ring and offers love and grace, helping mitigate and stabilize their high octane experience of life.

Both have made me a much better human by allowing me to walk with them in trusted trials and growing pains, gleeful victories and hard earned successes, discovering this kind of love as impervious and enduring. They have humored my retelling anecdotes of their childhoods with tolerant amusement and eye rolls, like a pension payout for having given birth to them. What an added gift to see them marry their absolute matches, two daughters-in-law I adore and highly esteem. It is a wise parent who steps into becoming extended family so your kids can form their own immediate families. I have never regretted encouraging this for them. Watching them thrive is deeply rewarding. Recently I've become a grandma, an absolute delight of a very different nature. I anticipate more writing to roll out of me in this new phase of life, but that is for another book.

Saying hello to newborns obviates saying goodbye to near adults launching, with countless hellos and goodbyes in between. We've blanketed ourselves in uncontainable laughter over these years, but of course there have been tears, undoubtedly more mine, as I've watched them grow and go. Our youngest chose college on the West Coast and stayed. Our oldest returned after college to Chicago and then shortly thereafter to New York City. Moving all those times myself didn't prepare me for being the one staying, without them, and the sure signs of these amazing men permeating our home. In 2023, one of them made a determined decision to move he and his wife to Israel. After prior years of short trips there, I thought I could manage this distance. That was true for the seven weeks before Hamas' attack on Israel on October 7th arrived. Being six thousand miles apart hit me like no other distance had–I felt helpless, scared, and wishing for some kind of unearthed superpower in me to bring them back to the safety of our family. Instead, I talked to God in choppy sentence prayers, reworked quasi-sovereign strategies to airlift them out of there, and cried more worried tears than I care to admit. Recently, they have returned to the US, more specifically to New York, leaving me awestruck by God's provision for our family to be reunited and doing life together. My best summary of this season is prayer sustains. God hears.

RAIN

How is it that life
Falls from the sky
In tiny droplets
Or pounding torrents
Waters everything
It touches

Grandma was afraid
Of storms
I was not—
Thanks to wise parents
Holding us close
And watching them
Talking about them
Together

I vowed the same
For my boys
Wrapped in blankets
On the screened porch
Sometimes
With hot chocolate
Excited shrieks
Following loud thunder
And flashes of lightning
In squeezy safe hugs

One didn't like it
On his face
Protesting loudly
I'd remind
Be glad it's not
Syrup or ketchup
Just rain
And you'll dry

The day came
Bikes were loaded
To ride back
After the van drop
At the mechanic's
The sky threatened
Fast approaching storm
We'd better hurry—
Too late

Riding to outrun
The pelting rain
Completely in vain
We succumbed
In giddy laughter
Quickly drenched
Sailing through deep
Instant puddles
Legs off the pedals
Soaked delight

How is it that life
Falls from the sky
Spontaneous storm
Lovingly embraced
Changes everything
It touches

05 December 23

LITTLE HAND IN THE DARK

I sleep lightly these days
Nights actually
Potty training is 24/7
At some point no diapers
Or they never learn
My youngest one calls me in the night
Mama, mama, go potty

I hear him hop out of bed
Feet padding to his doorway
I meet him in night's dim hall
Feel his little hand find mine
We walk to the bathroom
Little hand in the dark
I wait for him at the door

Neither of us speak
Until he says all done
Little steps toward me
Good job buddy
Feel his little hand find mine
We walk from the bathroom
Back to his room
Tired, yet I will miss this
His little hand in the dark

27 July 24

SUMMER FOR BOYS

Unshowered, ballcap covers messy hair
Sleep in clothes worn all day
Little matters but food and friends
Travel in packs looking for mischief
Making fun and memories unaware
Pegging balls and "shut up"
Mixed with Popsicles and burps
Candy wrappers and abandoned socks
Mental fistfights challenge the boy to become a man
Farmers tans and baseball
Sticks and rocks
Roadkill up close
Curiosity mingles with ripples of quiet fear
Learning life, soaking in lessons that root deeply
Skipping stones and muscle matches
Firecrackers and scaring cats
Video games, swimming, launching water balloons
Sleep till noon and lightning bugs
Let this linger forever…

04 July 08

REMEMBER

You tell me you don't remember
Your childhood very well
But I do
Recounting memories of you
They are diamonds in my mom crown
For whoever wants to see
They are perfect songs composed by love
For whoever wants to hear

You roll your eyes at your wife
When I sing again
One of those sweet melodic moments
From your early days
You've heard them before
But I don't care
Assuredly, I'll sing them again
Maybe even to your babies

Barely a mom
You'd fit into the curve of my neck
Like the found piece of a puzzle
Short newborn breaths
Not a care in your baby world
I'll hold you until you find your way
I tell myself to memorize this
Don't want to forget these moments
And you're too small to remember
So I will, for you

The first time you hugged me back
Little hands squeezing in a certain embrace
Barely eight months old
How did you know
Except hundreds had been yours
For your whole little life thus far

You'd pick the books before bedtime
The longest one I dreaded
But you loved it so
Sometimes I'd try to skip pages
Nothing got past you
Your mini protest would send me back
To read what was missed

Bedtime later by one half hour
Than your little brother
I hear you call "Mama"
After I've sat down to TV and popcorn
"I feel left out"

Ok little man I hear your heart
But not tonight – it's late
Another night we'll do this together
You're satisfied with this
And go right to sleep

You pair plaids with stripes
Wear winter gloves in summer
Red rain boots over bare feet
With a sweater vest as your baseball outfit
High red color in your cheeks
Playing hundreds of pretend big games
Little red t-ball bat and ball, beloved and scuffed
My dad's old mitt now yours too
You sleep with these
Like another kid's stuffed animal

The neighbor friend asks you
Who do you like more, me or her?
You wisely reply
I like you both the same amount
The boy across the street is trouble
You do your best to be his friend
Because that's who you are
Living out the blessing given
At your dedication, barely a month old

I'm warmed by these memories
Tiny time capsules
When opened make my heart burst
So unbelievably thankful
That I can remember them as I do
So thankful that I have always
Had all of these of you

21 December 23

LOVE, MOM

Before you even were
I fought for you to be
I wanted you to be
Who God designed
But I didn't know
I would become
So determined
To fight for you

In your early years
You had temper fits
I fought for you
To work it out
I prayed and sought counsel
I grew in patience
I loved you every day
Through every single fit

You broke your leg
I fought for you
To handle the body cast
And help you sleep
Endure pneumonia
And slowly heal
To stand and walk
And eventually run again

I also fought my boss
Who didn't understand
Why I would take six weeks
To be with you 24/7
If you were going through it
I'd go through it with you
I wasn't going to let you
Be alone in your pain

Then came the stomach aches
Many times a day you hurt
I fought for you
To get a diagnosis
That could be treated
And relieve your pain
Remember the day you finally
Weighed more than our dog?

Your young mind
Was beyond bright
I fought for the gifted group
But they couldn't see

Outside their box
Let alone see you
So together we walked away
From that fight

You had a new friend
Who provoked you and lied
To cover himself
I fought for you
For justice to emerge
And when it didn't
I wanted you to know
God and I believed you

Baseball had its troubles
I fought for you
Against ego-driven coaches
Who manipulated by fear
And stole the fun
From your beloved game
When you had enough
You bravely called it quits

When word hit the street
You weren't playing ball
I fought for you
To be given space
To try something new
You embraced lacrosse
Kissing baseball goodbye

You picked a documentary topic
Full of challenge
And controversy
I fought for you
To organize your thoughts
And produce a script
People could embrace
So God would be heard

And now here you are
Leaving for college
A new life chapter
There will be joys and trials
And more fights ahead
And I will be here
No matter what you need
Or what size the fight

For now I see
That God had a plan
To teach me through you
How to stand up
And call out justice
To not be afraid
Of whatever fight
Was in front of me

Together we've faced trials
Learned tough lessons
Gladly pursuing God's justice
And keeping the faith
I'm so very blessed
That you are my son
Don't ever forget
You are worth fighting for

Love,
Mom

16 August 2014

ROADTRIP

Semester ahead in Hollywood
The first week in January
Following a snowless Christmas
Midwest to West Coast
A rare chance to roadtrip with you
I gladly offered to co-pilot
Thinking of California's sun
As winter decidedly smirked

A cold day's travel without snow
Overnighting in North Platte
We departed for Denver
Majestic Rockies as the backdrop
Through Utah to the blue Pacific

Lunch and refueling in Golden
Tiny spits of snowflakes
Wafted down without notice
A call back home to report
Smooth sailing into the Rockies

The flakes became abundant
Barely a mile out of town
What started as inconsequential
Rapidly shifted to foreboding
As we climbed the mountains

Soon everything was blanketed
With heavy white coming at us
Skies unloading endless clumps
Like horizontal cotton balls
Robbing us of speed and visibility

I strained to see car tracks ahead
White knuckles gripping the wheel
As he downshifted the gear
Driving now demanding two people
Wide-eyed
Struggling to see 15 feet ahead
I donned my sunglasses to help
Moments later all was white

Heavy accumulating incline snow
Forcefully avalanched into our path
Leaving mere feet to swerve around
Nearly kissing the center parapet
Gutshock only added to the stress

Three hours became nine
We'll drive until they close the road
Pressing on into blinding white
Finally reaching a town for gas
Hardly anything open
Catch our breath, grab coffee
Return to the road under the thick falling snow

The weather shifted by Utah's border
From the band of wintry storms
To a clear dark starry night
Open roads and surrounding quiet
As if all had been a bad dream

No nighttime routines were followed
Collapsing into our hotel beds
We awoke still straining
To believe what we'd endured
How did we even make it through

Still to this day my worst snowstorm
Nothing has come even close
Our bond forged even deeper
I'd do it all again

04 August 25

NO ONE KNOWS

1:56am can't sleep
Stomach aching
Night is happening
All around me
No one knows
I'm awake

Two weeks left
Until he leaves
Keep myself busy
Packing boxes
No one knows
I'm dreading this

Eighteen years
Began with a breath
I can't catch mine
Tears choke me
No one knows
I can't breathe

We both will change
Everything will
And it won't
Change back
No one knows
I'm aching over this

I hear an owl
In the distance
He breaks my thoughts
Invades the stillness
No one knows
I'm listening

There is no comfort
In his calls
They simply remind
I am alone
No one knows
I'm not okay

And then it's quiet
Too quiet
Like my house
Will soon be
No one knows
I'm afraid

I've got to learn
This next lesson
I've got to step in
To this blank space
No one knows
I'm trembling

Take a moment
Pause and breathe
Expose these lies
Burdening me
Someone knows
I'm asking

Things are brighter
In the morning
So I must sleep
To get to tomorrow
God only knows
I'm trusting

All will be well
Be still and know
That He is God
And He is here
And He knows
I guess I'm not alone

03 August 14

SNOWY HALLOWEEN

First snowy Halloween
Just eight years old
When costumes were homemade
Or recycled from siblings
The princess mask I wore
Made my face sweat
Cracked around its edges
Head elastic's yellowing tape
Barely holding now
Where the nifty holes
Had long since broken off
Wet gown weighed down
Trampling through slush
And decayed icy leaves
This little royal maiden
Was over it

The second snowy Halloween
Old enough to trick or treat
Without grownups
Our 8th grade selves
Awkwardly couldn't decide
If we were just that cool
Or holding on to childhood
Raggedy bell bottoms
Colored Bandana
Pillowcase for the haul
Felt embarrassment
Grabbing at my soaked ankles
Go along with my friends
Laughter now my mask
This conflicted young girl secretly
Was over it

Another snowy Halloween
Sitting seat-belted on the tarmac
Plane in the de-icing line
Restlessly delayed takeoff
For Tuscan vineyards and Alps
Our 30th anniversary trip
Long awaited
Highly anticipated
The guy next to me
Ordered tea that arrived
After he fell asleep
Anxious to make it to JFK
In time for our connection
Couldn't mask my irritation
This 50-something wife
Was over it

This snowy Halloween
A mere four years later
I walk my furry old boy
Flurries melt on my glasses
Struggling to see
There's a war half the world away
Hamas has ripped off its mask
Two parts of my heart are there
One whose little hand I held
McDonald's pail of candy in mine
When his toddler legs grew weary
These past three weeks
Feel more like years
The snow falls coating the city
And this silver haired mama
Is over it

31 October 23

ROCKETS

The rockets red glare
Iron Dome intercepts
You text us at 1:33am
I wake up at 2:20am
I don't check messages
Any other night
But tonight I did
For some reason

You're staying put
No one's outside
Threat pends all day
And all night
You never know
When the alerts
Will cut the quiet
And send you
Into the stairwell

I see your face
On the video call
And you are stressed
Low affect yet vigilant
I want to scoop you up
Whisk you out of there
But this isn't my war
I have no power

The invisible shield
Can only do so much
It's better for me
To trust God Himself
And not go in my head
To that bad neighborhood
I'm tempted to visit
Which is purely a choice
I decide against over and over

You tell me
It's worse for me
And my imagination
But there's powder
And a firestorm
Falling on Gaza
And shrapnel
Everywhere else
I hate this

How long will this last?
Honestly it's been years
Until they pulled the pin
And now it's here
No one knows
Only God knows
The living
And the dead

Tether my soul
To faith and my family
And kindred friends
You tell me to call anytime
So I do and it helps
My inner tremor
Feels like rockets
I too need an Iron Dome

08 October 23

SHRAPNEL

Bombarding blasts
Of people posting comments
Like the rockets of war
Perhaps hoping they will land
And make a huge impact
For those in closest proximity
Maybe their intent
Isn't really destruction
But still their words do damage

I am weary
From pontifications
Targeting platforms
To serve as launchers
Sending into the cosmos
Sharp, pointed words
Some will experience these
As rockets and cheer
Others will cry in deep grief
And others will pay no attention
Until it hits them

But for me?
For me, my head is a storm
I can't see through the clouds
But I hear things
Falling from the sky
And landing all around me
I really hate the fallout
Whatever opinion you were hoping
Would make a big impact
To me
It's only shrapnel

12 October 23

DROWN OUT

Flight attendant motions
Safety guidelines
But I've muted her
AirPods in and loud
To drown out my thoughts
You just witnessed
A rocket interception
Thank you
Iron Dome
But I am tremoring
Again
And I hate all of this
You were my baby
27 years ago
But right now
I'm just as frail
As I was in delivery

Swallow the tears
Challenge my fears
The song plays
Unexpected words
"I'm not alone in this"
I know the next lyrics
"The best is yet to come"
So I hold on tightly
To hope and abiding love
I think I cannot do this
But God
Yet God
Surrounds me

This will be an interminable flight
Taking only two hours
But until I can call again
It's dreadfully long
I hear your voice
In my head
As you retell your trauma
I know I gave you help
But I'm only human
We need the transcendent
The eternal rescuer
To hold us
And protect us

I struggle to recall
Where I am presently,
This connecting location,
I know my destination
But it's all scrambled
Momentarily
This too shall pass
But until it does
I'm suspended
In the claustrophobic now

God intercept
These thoughts
And intense feelings
Calm my frame
Allow me to breathe
Filtered cabin air
Until I land
Back on the ground
Flight attendant
Please stop talking
So I can quiet
My tender mama's soul

13 October 23

ALWAYS IN LOVE

You took your first steps
Up the stairs of this life
You started together
A few years back
I've watched you both
Sometimes close up
Sometimes from afar
But always in love

How does it feel
To build this life together
As best of friends
As biggest fans
Knowing and being known
Home and being home
But always in love

And now here you are
Stepping soon
Into a new room
Of this life
As a mom and a dad
Soon your baby girl
Will tiptoe, spin and twirl
Around your hearts
Into your world
Deep, deep delight
Always in love

23 December 23

FIRST BABY GIRL

A dollhouse and play kitchen
Tutus and slippers
Pinks and purples and roses
Jewelry and tiaras
Mary Jane patent leathers
Skirts and tights
Tiny little purses
It's all headed our way
Arriving with our first
Grandbabygirl
So teach me little one
All your joy, all your fun

14 February 24

WHILE BABY SLEEPS

Little fingers
Little toes
Dark brown hair
Perfect nose

I hold you close
Much to tell
Your mama rests
All is well

It's quiet now
Time just creeps
I fall in love
While baby sleeps

13 July 24
Sealed with KZ

BIRTHDAY

Warm breezy afternoon
Beloved Riverside Park
In our Big Apple
Picnic table spread with food
You can feel the joy

My first and his first
Born on the same day
We gather to celebrate
Relish the gift this is
We're all here together

Little one takes it all in
Happy to sit in my arms
She's one today
Eyes wide with wonderment
First taste of cake

He wears a crown
Like storybook Max
He is equally quite the king
Embodying delight
Let the wild rumpus begin

We revel in today
Holding fast this treasure
Gathered from near and far
Unknown are the ones ahead
One by one, happy birthday

28 June 25
Sealed with J&L.

CHAPTER 6:

I entered college as a Music Business major hoping to run the business side of music recording, but when I learned how many Econ courses were ahead for me, I started looking for another gig. Girls on my floor often popped their heads in my door to talk, shared some struggle they were carrying, or sought out the welcome of our room when feeling lonely. I don't remember who, but one of them said, "You ought to be a shrink or something," the idea of which struck a chord in me. I had no idea what was involved in becoming a "shrink or something," but soon consulted with my college advisor, who guided me through a change of major. What I didn't know at the time was that I was exchanging Econ classes for Stats classes as a Psych major, a truly cruel trick to play on an aspiring therapist.

The fall of my senior year I was looking into grad schools and not excited about the programs available at the time. On the eve of my GRE exam, I decided I wasn't going to apply to begin that next fall. This served as both a pressure release valve and some sort of comfort to wait until I found a program that fit me. Student loan debt and coursework fatigue steered me to work for a year and start looking for a faith-integrated grad program. By now faith was an anchor for me and I was becoming disenchanted with psychology as a stand-alone discipline. Learning that seminaries had counseling programs was a delightful find—a perfect fit for me to gain equal footing in Psychology and Theology. This would fulfill my end goal to become a Christian Counselor and I loved the masters program immensely. I was finally finding my career path, or more aptly, it was finding me.

After seminary graduation, I had to gain employment to accrue hours for the licensure exam. I chartered the private practice route, in spite of professors ney saying. I wasn't interested in social service agencies after a college internship with child protective services. Supervising visits with abusive parents was miserable; I still think of those kids with sadness. My first job was in a private Christian practice, my second job was in a private Christian practice, my third and current job is owning my own private Christian practice. To this day, I think that's pretty cool.

Being a Christian Counselor is a bit of a peculiar thing, integrating faith with clinical training. Here I am recognized as a state-licensed therapist who draws upon and utilizes faith supports as a meaningful strategy for growth and freedom alongside evidence-based treatments. I consider myself eclectic in my therapeutic approach as there are many wonderful methodologies to custom tailor positive counseling outcomes. Humanity is plagued with many forms of brokenness, both externally and internally, causing varying levels of discomfort and distress. This reality obviates the need for a variety of strategies to employ for relief. Focusing my practice in grief, loss, trauma, and life adjustments also means that I see a wide array of clients experiencing differing forms of pain. I marvel at the breadth of counseling needs that come through my door and sit on the couch: child loss, violent crimes, on-the-job traumas, incarcerations, relationship failures, cancer diagnoses, suicide attempts, and the list goes on.

How satisfying it is to find relief and healthy well-being when we integrate a variety of strategies in the therapeutic process. I still truly love this work after more than thirty years as a therapist.

I've been asked many times how I handle dealing with people's problems all the time, a common misunderstanding of this field. I often begin my answer with how much I really love people and carry a resident fascination with their unique expressions of personality! I am regularly wowed by the people I get to work with, watching them grow into wiser and more secure versions of themselves. Second, understanding that problems aren't mine to carry serves as a necessary launchpad to hand them over to The Creator. We aren't built to be a bottomless repository for someone else's pain.

I am also glad to share that putting myself in counseling to contend with my own dysfunction has been such a freeing gift. I am thankful for the therapists who have allowed me to be the client and face my own losses and lean into deeper channels of growth. Finally, finding ways to process the weight of this work is essential. We all need healthy ways to feel and think about the gravity of one's human experience. Writing has been a significant way to cope throughout my years as a counselor. While it's taken years to evolve, processing via poetry has helped me metabolize events or emotions that were staying with me longer than usual. Once composed, a resulting poem became a comforting record for me to reflect and digest life.

THE CALLING SWING

A day away, age 23
Doing as I would often do
Big decisions like chain mail
Bearing weight on my shoulders
Retreat of silence
A discipline from college
Time to breathe
Time to pray

The thoughts of future
Way out in front of this day
Are creeping closer
Hard to ignore
I need some space
To hear from God
So I get in the car

The usual places of retreat
Are states away
Explore new roads
To quiet sanctuaries
Discover bird symphonists
Amid leaves clapping for joy
Whose branches raise in praise
As the nearby brook waterfalls

No one is here — perfect —
As if placed by Heaven itself
An inviting wooden roped swing
On a sturdy muscled branch
I'll sit here for unmeasured time
What do you want me to do God?
I am stalled
Without your push and prompt

Inaudibly you speak
If I dare trust, follow through
To counsel singly aligned with you
Not a career, but a deeper calling
My resonating soul hears
What my mind questions
A tender invitation
Outranks anything of occupation

Shift from sitting tiptoe to dirt
To lifting and pumping
Back and forth, to and fro
Like I did as a child
Higher with each motion

Higher now with emotion
It's a dream meant for reality
You lovingly send me skyward

If I have any peace
It's in this
Your quiet yet bold soul speak
Sings over me and into me
I won't forget this
Many decades later
This place, this moment
The calling swing

31 March 24

GOODBYE INTERRUPTED

He was awful to her
The kids chimed in
She hid in her room
Broken and alone

No sleep last night
No peace
No one
To console her

And so the day began
They left for the day
And she was
Alone

Her mind began
To plan her end
Gathering
And counting
The deadly pills

She took the pen
To write her goodbye
Amid tears
She heard inside
"Call Joy"

No strength to call
She texted instead
I'm at the end
I just want to sleep
Forever
But I heard
"Call Joy"

The brief words
Stunned me
Cut into me
This one I've thought of
And prayed for
Seven months have passed

How does one
At her end
Still hear God
And stop her end?
A humbling miracle
God is strong
And

God is loud
And
God is Love

Such deep love
To reach her
In the depths
Of despair
And draw her out
God is Love

He loves me too
With this great love
I don't deserve
I don't understand
Why such love?
Why call me?
I am broken also

I couldn't text
Instead I called
Distraught
She answered
But she answered!
A second miracle

And so we talked
She sobbed
She told her story
God was with us
God gave wisdom
God is strong

Are you willing
To flush the pills?
You have to be safe
The pills aren't
Your answer
The One who said
"Call Joy"
Is your answer

We both must trust
God Himself
And God in each other
He is here
And
He loves you

Tonight she's safe
Tucked with care
In a safe place
Now it's time
To rest and heal
God is strong
And
God is Love
And
She is alive –
She is not dead

19 November 12

REFUGE

hundreds of people
thousands of hours
millions of words
countless tears
secrets shared
wounds revealed
smiles found
reassurances given
tissue boxes
pens
so many pens
copious casenotes
endless cups of coffee
books loaned
scriptures revisited
memories
God does his best work
when we are broken

FUNERAL

Today is your funeral
I don't want to get out of bed
Instead I'm laying here
Thinking
Of the hours we talked
Of the tears you cried
Of the things you said

I see your face
I hear your voice
Crack from the pain
Your broken heart
Didn't have to happen
But it did
And we went over that
Many times

I know the stats
One in two chances
Of getting sick
After too much stress
Your heart told us so
Two months ago
And you came back
Determined to live

But then your heart
Let her back in
And it was good
For a few weeks
Until something shifted
And she left you
A second time
And it was worse
Than the first time

Everything converged
In less than a week
Divorce papers
The night before you'd
Walk your daughter down the aisle
And kiss her goodbye
We didn't know
It was truly goodbye

So three days out
We sat and looked back
Recounting it all
And then turning

To look ahead
Still wondering
If you feared loneliness
Or just life without her

Still determined
To live
We said our goodbyes
You mentioned
The good Lord
And I promised
We'd talk more of Him
Next time

48 hours later
Your heart broke
Once and for all
And you left us
You left all the pain
Behind too
Good for you
Go to the place
Where there is no sorrow

'Next time'
Those words haunt me
Knowing it won't be
On this side
My heart is broken
For what was
And will never be again

I read through my notes
Last night
And cried
Looking for missed hints
And cried some more
This morning
Working to steady myself
Before I see your shell
And say for the last time
Goodbye

ON THE NIGHT OF NO NEXT WEEK

Here I sit with tears again
How many have fallen
This week
I can't count
But this is grief
And it comes in waves
In memories
In images in my mind
In knowing this is it

It's been a long time coming
And I stand on the edge
Of next things
Unknowns
Wonder
And
My heavy heart

I want to take it all
With me
Somehow packing it
Into a perfect box
That has no bottom
And the farther I reach
The deeper it goes
Til I grasp
Something
From long ago

The ribbon wrapped pen
With a flower end
The pottery nail-pierced hand
The card with a name in LA
The scripture box with lid
The baby pictures
The cards of thanks
The tissues
The tears
The verses
The sunsets
And every single precious life

Talk of the unchangeable past
Deep wrestlings of today
Tomorrow's too distant reach
I wish you'd just tell me what to do
Why did God let this happen
Betrayals
Broken lives
Cancers and heart attacks

And little kids without dads
Mothers without their babies
And the weight of sin
The endless questions why
And the deeper things
Of God
It's all packed

This has always been His
I have always been His
They have always been His
He put all the fallen tears
In his bottle
He took every prayer
Every word
Every thought
Every question
Every plea and bargain
Every breath
To himself for safe keeping
And so I rest
I trust
I breathe
On the night of no next week

25 February 21

RELEASE

Today your sentence
Is over
You've served
Your time
25 months
11 days
6 hours
8 minutes
Over

How to begin
Outside this
Cement hell
Locked cell
Inhumane place
Once you're released
Who will detect
Your invisible prison
Even when free?

It takes a long time
To shed the prison garb
The constricted self
The demoralized man
The forgotten boy
The lonely son
The broken soul
And believe
You are unlocked
Free to move about
Unless you choose
The shackles again

26 September 23

FAIRY GODMOTHER

Not to be dramatic
But she came into my life
Kicking and screaming
Confessing deep hatred
Insinuating murder
For all who had harmed her
And she had been HARMED—
That word alone
An egregious understatement
I wait for her to be avenged
In eternity

We covered years
Sometimes within minutes
What happened to her in minutes
Was spread over hours
Of gut wrenching sessions
Unpacking boxes of broken pieces
Fragments and slivers
Of her worth
Her self-esteem
The still smoldering ashes
Of her person
Burned down senselessly
By the people in her life
Also known as Family

Not to be dramatic
But it took her literally years
To trust me, to believe me
When I refuted every time
Her apologies for bothering me
When I reminded every time
I wasn't going anywhere
When I remained every time
She wanted to end it all
When the terrified child inside
Emerged from what appeared
To be the shell of an adult
Frozen with fear I'd abandon her
Looking up in disbelief that I hadn't
It took years of proving my words
Actions repeated over and over
Before the seeds of trust took root

Not to be dramatic
But the highest praise she gave
Was choosing to rename me *friend*
She'd only had one other

In the muck of her burdened life
Her trust was golden and pure
More delicate and intricate
Than most forms otherwise
She understood the boundaries
Yet still chose to refer to me
As *friend*, not just her counselor

My colleagues said lose her
She is a high liability
With her intractable suicidality
There's no way to calculate
When, not if, but when
My practice partner asked
If I would let her go
Not a chance
He smiled in full agreement

Her desire to live changed
With a cancer diagnosis
I watched her decide to stay
Fight for what little she had
The chemo asked far more
Of her than her psych meds
Still she knew her limits
Foregoing the long term
To survive the short term
I can't do both right now

The cancer abused her
Time and time again
I sat with her at death's door
As she asked if she was going to die
I've never lied to you, so yes
I held her hand
Because we both knew
The life she had planned to take
Was now taking her
We said our tearful goodbyes

She quietly slipped away
Into that promised eternity
Two very long days later
I got the call
Reduced to tears upon disconnect
This one who had asked for help
Helped me far far more
Not to be dramatic

05 May 24

BIG BUS

I see your tears falling as
You sit across from me
On the double decker
We are surrounded
With grand architecture
Historical palaces
Bright sun
And people
On the street below

I hand you
What tissues I have
Tenderly smiling
So you know
I see you
Whatever hurts
Matters
To this counselor
To this American in Paris

I silently pray all will be well
For your pain
I look away
To give you privacy
No one likes
To be watched
While crying
But you thank me
As I descend the stairs

21 August 23

NOT LOST ON ME

Your hard work
Started as pain
Your visible growth
Came from thirst
Aching hunger
Needing sunlight
Where once
There was darkness
Loneliness
Disqualifying yourself
Believing lies
Filled with insecurity
Mistrust
Fear
Shame

I've watched you
Reach for truth
Embrace it
Hold on for dear life
Refusing to let go
Of what you've gained
Making it yours
Sharing it with others

I've seen you
Struggle and fight
The good fight
Knowing that good
Will rescue you
And deliver you
To a place of peace
Freedom
Expansive pasture

You are to me
That field of wildflowers
Colorful in verdant grasses
Moved by gentle breeze
Arms welcoming sun
A place of beauty
For all to behold

You are to me
Healing embodied
With reminding scars
That all is now well
Where once
There were deep cuts
Inflicted by another

You are to me
The cheerful receiver
Of an also cheerful gift
One that is sweeter
Because you trusted
A grace of sorts
Unavailable
To one who refuses

Your words and tears
Are not lost on me
Falling on tender soil
Encouraging
My own growth—
Delight is deeper
Because of you
Gratitude and joy
Forever ours

28 February 24

TONIC AND LIME

Long day
Beats me up
Spits me out
Worse for wear
They all leaned in
I held it up
For them

Who's in my
Pocket tonight
Scoop me up
Let me be weak
If just for a brief
Set of moments
Let me cry

Thirty years
Mostly shiny
Some a bit scratched
Yet I've loved it
But tonight
Some nights
I don't

It would be gold
To come home
To you
So easily known
Lock on my eyes
Rush to embrace
My ashes

You show up
In different forms
My adoring person
Loud music
Comforting verses
But tonight
You are tonic and lime

21 Sept 23

MOST OF ALL

I've sat in the darkest places
With those completely undone
Lives unraveled
In an instant
By the choice of another
Sadly it was a choice
Though this may sound harsh—
No one forced them to decide
No one was there
To make sure it happened
Instead they were gone
From life to death
Just like that

I've sat in the aftermath
With families drowning
In a sea of questions
All unanswered
With no chance
Of one that satisfies
It's endlessly lonely
Perpetually undoing
Deeply jarring
Like few other things
We could ever face

How did you get to that moment?
How did this become
Your most viable option?
Did you pause in that sacred gap
Of consciousness
Before acting
On your choice?
I would hope you thought
About the ones you're leaving
The ones you're leveling
The ones you're devastating
The ones you're killing
Who will remain alive
In a suspended
Excruciating
Existence
A shell of the person
They once were

I know it's not this simple—
A most complicated mess
Sifting through thoughts
Agonizing over and over

Repeating questions
Reworking options
Overthinking to exhaustion
Is there any other way
To be able to stay?
My compassion
Runs directly into
Your mile-thick cobweb of pain
I'm so sorry
This is where you ended
I'm so gutted
For both the dead
And the living
Cast in this pall
Honestly I hate suicide
Most of all

04 January 24
Sealed with DB

I CAN'T SEE TO THE OTHER SIDE

I can't see to the other side
The gray crashing waves
On the Great Lake
Feel like an ocean to me
An expanse I cannot traverse
At least not for now
After yesterday
So unexpectedly
She collapsed
Into your everlasting arms
And you carried her
Into the forever of eternity

My finite self
Cannot comprehend
The infinite
Faith cradles me
In this temporary shell
Protects me
Amidst this jarring news
Expected tears didn't arrive
Until hours later
Then began the flood
And a fitful night of sleep
Did I even sleep?

Cold, gray winter rain
Falls on frozen ground
Unable to absorb
All that falls from the sky
And the news from the call
That she is gone
Equally hard to absorb—
We texted the day before
Her last words to me
Thanks for keeping me healthy
Neither of us knew
How profound those words were
But now they serve
As the most fitting epilogue
For the final chapter
Of the last book

A complete anthology
Of hours, words, feelings
And questions
Infrequently buttoned up
But her heart was open
Full of light and life

Volume after volume
Now beautifully bound
An unseeable treasured collection
I fill this new sixth shelf
With her beloved books
No one prepared me for this—
Five complete sets already
One for each I've lost
Throughout my career

I look at the whole of these
Recalling countless hours
Pouring through chapters
Of life and loss
They each so kindly offered
Me to read
Now I reflect on the words
Indelibly penned
On my heart and mind
No one else to cipher
What was written
In invisible ink
What a privilege
To be the keeper
Of this hidden library

Still I look up
From this most recent book
To the grayest of days
Out my window the fog and mist
Match my sad heart
Visibility so low
Her absence struggles
To settle into my mind
Like walking on rocks—
If eternity is a stone's throw
It remains a place I've yet to hike
Quietly reminding myself
I can't see to the other side

GOOD ADVICE

She came asking for good advice
The only thing to give without a BA
All nineteen years of her
To my twenty-one
Her own disbelieving gloating
Mixed with an imagined relationship
With a flirtatious boy
Who'd never choose her
But dined on her ego strokes
Drank her loyal unrequited attention

I too easily read that room
How he toyed with her adoration
I played out for her
Several honest iterations
None would make him hers
But she could walk away intact—
Denial bigger than her dream
She heard what she wanted
Left the rest at the door
Trotting off to do the opposite
Of what she asked me to advise

Many years later post college
I learned she had ended her life
Supposedly her exit
From an abusive marriage
To someone cut off
The same bolt of cloth
As her college fantasy
Leaving a little boy motherless
Her adoring parents reeling
This present therapist angry
Recounting her college choices

More recently I found myself
Out for dinner, ambushed
Under the ruse of friendship
I'm met with similar disbelief
And that all too familiar gloating
Incredulous she's been asked
To resign her moral post
Because her mismatched romance
Flies in the face of her faith walk

She touts spiritual maturity
While revealing her childish ways
Claiming innocence—
She won't receive it as counsel
Instead reduces it to good advice

With no intention of taking heed
Of the truth she's hearing
Of letting him find his way
Of giving it time's test

She falls over herself thanking me
Saying now so much to consider
Giving gratuitous lip service
To her new enlightened perspective
It sounds genuine—
Sadly instead it resembles
Colored mashed potatoes
Photographed as ice cream
An unbending scoop of her will
That will never melt

No surprise she's engaged
After a month of shoreline sunsets
Have passed since our heavy dinner
After very few months of dating
Leaving truth again at the door
Denial greater than her dream
There's no way a life converts
And matures that quickly
But the setting by the lake
And on her finger
Is oh so magical to some

I feel sadness where they felt joy
Like I did in college about that boy
Playing her with no plan of loving her
A girl smitten, disregarding flags
Now here yet another
She'll walk down the aisle
Carpeted with counterfeit hope
They both just wanted the man
Not truth that is worth gold
Good advice is cheap and tarnishes

Some truly seek wisdom and care
As incongruent relationships
Burden their tender souls
Steal freedom and delight
I'll walk alongside them any day
Investing time and my full attention
But for those seeking approval
To dance the self-destructive road
I bid them farewell, watch them go
Grabbing on their way out the door
Easily disposable good advice

COLD COFFEE

Cup of coffee
And half a sandwich
No appetite—
Hugs
And tears
And questions
Sooo many questions
I too am lost
And scared
By all their thoughts
And questions

Could anyone know what I'm
Thinking
Feeling
Imagining
If I'm completely honest
I want to push it away
Restart the clock
Wave a wand
Make it disappear
Make it all go away

I watch them
Bewildered
Lost
Angry
Broken hearted
Reaching for arms
And answers
And directives
For life from here on
What are we going to do?
This unsettles me too

Teachers aren't supposed to die
Let alone take their own life
Undoing all the good
They were doing
Shaping impressionable minds
Including my own sons
So now it's also personal
This is a complete mess

Think, don't feel, for now
You can feel it all later—
Promise yourself you'll feel
The depth and breadth of this
When you have space

But for now it's go time
Work to stabilize the sand
We're all left straddling

All day long
I sit with them
Groups of kids
Colleagues
Individuals
Administration
Confusion abounds
For every person
How do I measure
This was good work?
Hours later
I make my way back
To that same cup
Of now cold coffee

September 2013

THIS IS WHY

This is why I keep inventory
Making available to others
Something once held only by me
This is why I sometimes sift through
In a sacred nanosecond
Files upon years of files
From my memory drawers
Looking to see if useful today
Surprisingly easily reopened
Brought out into fluorescent light
Illuminating my life's office
Recounted here and now

This is why taking out one memory
Makes room for others
To shift in their place and space
Resultantly more accessible
Exposing its bent corner
Now grabbing my attention
My recall reaches for it
Saying oh yes, I know this moment
Unsure there'd be a use for it
But here it is, fitting the immediate

The copious drawers of files
Undeniably prove
I am a collector of memories,
The rich and varied tapestry
Of life experiences,
Mental snapshots,
Treasures I wanted to keep
Seemingly worth saving at the time
Even if just for my own future
Perusal and enjoyment
Yet then again
Maybe for somebody else someday
At a perfectly curated moment

I've seen it happen time and again
Something dog-eared pops up
Drawn upon to share with another
Whose life might make more sense
Because of this prior filed moment
Now being brought to the table
With an invitation to taste and see
If it might help fill the soul's hunger

It wasn't encouraged to self-disclose
In our graduate training,
In fact, our lives were something
To be daintily tucked away
Minding our trim therapeutic waist
Only to be retrieved as a tiny sliver
On a china plate with lace napkin
You'd never wipe your mouth with
Unless it was clinically necessary
Perhaps remotely helpful
It's decorum barely visibly ruffled

But I'm the kind of person
Who cuts an oversized slice instead
Puts it on a plate with two forks
We'll partake together
We'll chew on and savor
I'm generous in those servings
Of disclosures
I really don't care
What my professors would say
A few of them now dearly departed
I wonder how much they abided
By that training rule?
Did they ever deviate, like myself
To engage in a rich
Delightful morsel of connection?
To make something nondescript
More digestible and fulfilling
The taste of which now pleases
Someone's previously troubled palate

So if you're wondering
The substance of one's life
The recollection collection's value
Dare to retrieve your own
Delectable store of the forgotten
There are certainly exquisite
Offerings to sample and consider
Someone else might find so perfect
When you kindly retrieve it
Place it on a plate with two forks
Surprised it surfaced, so apt
Nourishing you both
Feeding the soul
This is why

CHAPTER 7:

No memoir would be complete without some account of loss and death. We spend much of life denying or avoiding its reality, hoping to squeeze out extra years with kale smoothies and cardio in order to enjoy retirement, travel and grandkids. This chapter is my confirmation of Henry Wadsworth Longfellow's poetic line, "Into each life some rain must fall." Oh how the rain has fallen in my heart over the course of my life, and surprisingly, I am better for it. While I may be a grief, loss and trauma therapist by trade, I am more qualified by personal experience. Let me explain.

Both of my parents died in their 84th year, my mom unexpectedly preceding my dad by six and a half years, because she was older than him by the same. I was 46 when mom died three days after a massive stroke, an age I was sure was too young to be burying a parent. I had already devastatingly lost her mom when I was 18, a cruel catapult into loss before I barely knew who I was, and certainly had no preparation for a world without her. These women provided an alliance of influence for me, neither having education beyond the twelfth grade, they taught me life skills and peoplesmarts I carry with me to this day.

Mom was a prize-winning pie baker, I feel proud every time I make a great pie knowing she would've loved it. She was a Depression era baby, able to stretch a dollar and saved everything for a future use, often much to my vexation. She was cleverly creative with crafts and homemaking, taught two-year olds in Sunday school memory verses, was witty and fun-loving, competitive at board games, carried out a wealth of fun surprises, and made sure I knew how much she loved me. Sometimes her words and even remnants of her voice roll out of my own mouth, comforting and amusing me. While I've written about my grandma in earlier parts of this book, she was everything a little girl could love, with mesmerizing back scratches, playing cards, Dum dum suckers as rewards, the best laugh when humored, and the "purse" for special gifts and celebration dinners a pastor's salary couldn't afford. She was the keeper of my secrets and reminded me often how much she loved and enjoyed me. Losing them still hurts at times, though the best of them always remain in my memories.

Dad was acquainted with grief at an early age, his mom dying when he was fourteen. This shaped him in irreversible ways, developing an obsession with order, personal grooming, proper attire and manners, perhaps each as a means to cope when things felt out of his control. He was the embodiment of a gentleman, opening doors and helping us don our coats, buying Valentine cards for us signed just from him, and praising whoever cooked an amazing meal, because he loved good food more than anyone I've known. He was a man of severe conscience and deep faith, filing as a military Conscientious Objector and enduring arduous proceedings to be granted that status. As a CO, he was assigned to work at the county hospital, soon after contracting tuberculosis and sent to a TB Sanitarium for six months of treatment and recovery. His being away from my mom and his newly adopted sons (my half brothers) was difficult on everyone.

Sixty years later, he began battling what he thought was a recurrence of TB, but was unfortunately diagnosed with lung cancer instead. For six months he denied the reality of the disease while I painfully watched his obstinate faith serve as proof he was "'healed.'" The cancer grew in spite of chemotherapy and snuffed out hope for recovery. We opened our home to him for hospice care and he died less than 24 hours after arriving, another abrupt loss I added to my grief pack. Losing him was complicated; I work to embrace all of the good he instilled in me, am forever indebted to him for my deep roots of faith, and fondly recall his earlier affirmations of me as a competent woman whom he respected and loved.

Loss doesn't solely come in human form. We often invite God's creatures into our homes and hearts, sometimes more easily than people. While I had many pets growing up, my dad would often rehome them before we moved, a practical task before loading the moving truck. It wasn't until I was a parent myself that I shopped for our first pet named Otto, an Australian cattle dog for my son's seventh birthday, who lived to the end of his first year of college. Seven weeks later we were adopting Oakley, an F1 Goldendoodle, because my younger son insisted the house was too quiet and lonely without a dog. Oakley was with us nearly 14 years, a loss I'm still grieving as I write this book.

Having recently entered my sixties, with none of us knowing our determined days, it seemed time to get this body of work to the printers. I'm not guaranteed the sum of eighty-four years myself like my parents were given. While I dearly love my life as it unfolds, I do greatly look forward to wrapping up this finite life when God decides and becoming infinite in eternity with Jesus. That will be my life's longest desire fulfilled. Until then, I will faithfully press on, trusting I've lived this life given me on purpose.

GEM

If grief was my necklace
You are the gem
Encased in gold
Laying closest to my heart

In loss, you were my first
In pain, you were my worst
In family, you were the dearest
In life, you were the nearest

I've carried you close
From girlhood to gray
Holding my granddaughter
You're here in me, today

Once upon a time
That was you and me
I anxiously await our reunion
Someday in eternity

11 Sept 24
For Grandma

THE ROAD IS LONG

Room filled with mixed conversations
Scatters of tears and laughter
You move to adjust your comfort
Or let us know you're still with us
You don't seem to care for the truth
That brought you here
Got us here
Keeps us here
Brings more family here

The road is long
Countless steps through life
And days
And years
And memories
And now breaths
Leading closer to this coming intersection
I don't want this
I know you are mixed too
I wish I could read your mind
You've given me millions of hints
But I still can't break the code
Only God knows what can't be known
I'm going to have to surrender
So are you
But you have a party waiting
I have a funeral—
Or a celebration if we can manage

The road is long
I don't know how to follow you
Or get there yet
All I have is a map
That unfolds day by day
And now by moment
By breath

I want to memorize everything I've missed
So do you I know
And yet we've been given a gift
To walk this road together
For 46 years
and nine months
And more I wish now so badly

The road is long
And you get to go ahead

But not alone
Never alone
He promised
You told me so
I believe it
I believe you
And I love you

The road rises up to meet you
I'll be along soon
However long soon is
I don't know
But God knows
And I can accept that
God will help me
God will help you

03 September 10
For Mama

GIFT CARD

She was always saving
For a rainy day
Depression baby that she was
A small amount of cash
She would happily tuck away
Or a check sent as a gift
She would keep as equity

In the sunset of her life
Came a new thing to save
Neatly boxed gift cards
Held onto like gold
Her dream of using them
At some point in the future
Entertained her wishful self

Yet it was always the same
Stash them away
In a little cardboard box
Promising someday
Something special
Something she'd been wanting

This went on
For a very, very long time
Celebrated accumulations
Of wedding and funeral stipends
My preacher dad gave her
All in the little white box
Amid her underwear and socks

I'd forgotten them
Figured she'd spent them
Certain the time came
When she gathered them
Put them to good use
Once that perfect thing
Came along

I never asked – just assumed
They were spent with delight
I mean who wouldn't?
She had plans for them
She had plans for herself
Years stacked on years
Dreams on top of dreams

Sorting through her things
The week after her funeral
What to donate
What to pass on
What to keep—
There was so much stuff
Take a breath, elbow deep

Because she couldn't
Ever make up her mind
Hundreds of choices
Now were mine
Yet lovingly stowed away
There it was – from years before
The little white box
In her top shallow drawer

Imagine my heart dropping
As I lifted its lid
Though married with children
I felt once again little myself
Then just as quickly
I felt a bit jarred
Here the outdated checks
Every treasured gift card

23 Feb 24
Sealed with DaKris

GRAVESIDE

We never seemed to bury
Our loved ones
The day of their funerals
The elongated pause
Before final goodbyes
Was weeks after
I never liked this

Every time was hard
But this one was harder
The final goodbye
Placing her ashes there first
In the tiny vertical hole
Somehow we're to make this
Their final resting place

Losing my mom hurt—
She was our glue, gone now
Surrounded by us
Her lineage
Four generations
Gathered in solemnity
No one held hands

It came like a flood
Timber log emotions
Splintering into pieces
Gaining speed in seconds
I stood there sobbing
Really, truly sobbing
All the years were now tears

Sadder still was to realize
No one came around me
No hands or arms to grasp
Instead a stifled "let's go"
All of them stoically retreated
For me, something else died
There at her graveside

09 June 25
Sealed with JME

BROTHER

He was gone
By the time I knew
He was even there
Nineteen years
Separated us
And lots of drink

He angered easily
And overreacted
Scared me
Hurt me
Embarrassed me
Discarded me

He made promises
He never planned
To keep
Never remembered
My little heart
Or my hopes
That he'd make good
On his words

And he hurt his kids
Sometimes with his hand
And always
With his fury
So they cowered
And backed away

Life went on
Barely–
We loved him
But he could not
Receive
He repelled
So walled off

Tragedy
Didn't change him
Love
Didn't free him
Death
Took him

But he was dead
Long before that
And we couldn't
Revive him

Can good be found?
Redeeming love
Somewhere
Way back there
Had a name
Yes she loved him
To the end

And she met him
When last breaths
Escaped
Leaving behind
An empty shell
She took his hand
And walked him home

Now he's free
And I've forgiven
His offenses
Without receiving
Apology
Or compassion
Oddly providing
That I too
Am now free

08 September 12

ER

A set of revolving doors
And beds
And people
I've been here before
I didn't want to be here then
Or now
But I am
Babies too little to say where it hurts
Rush of medics and gurneys
Code A stage 3 Room 8
Tears and tissue boxes
Machines for tests
Results in hushed tones
Cell phones ring
Call lights ding
No sound sleep
And so we wait
And wait
Meeting shifts of nurses
Like changing of the guard
For a room in the ICU
It's been over a day
Without night
For I could not sleep
He rests with shallow snore
Between blood draws
Drips empty and need replacing
Meds keep the heart
From attacking once more

11 February 12

TWO YEARS

here i am
and you aren't
i hurt quietly
don't expect this
to hit radars
of others

just me
missing you
wanting to see you
hear your voice
see you smile

tell me i'll be alright
tell me it gets easier
tell me to hang on
i would believe you
you are now perfect
and i am not

dad felt you with him
i want that too
my friend tells me
you are with me
i want to believe that
but no clear sign

thought you were
in the swirling smoke
at fireside last week
but still i want
more
of you
sure signs
you're with me

i hear you
in my words
i find you
in my head
i see you
in my mind
but i want you
here
just here
with me

04 September 12

DEATHBED

We hardly made the bed
Before he died in it
The hours in between
A brutal spiritual assault
Perpetual faith abrasions
Grasps losing grips
Writhing in torment
Fighting to the death

I said I'd never speak of this
Never considered I'd pen
A thorn pricking my recall
Urging I verbalize
The warping nature of transition
Opening my sadness
For the world to read
From lifelong breath to death

It was a slow gradual decline
Death perhaps beginning
When his beloved succumbed
I witnessed the invisible
Decay of his known heart
Mind expiring over six years
Thought by unvoiced thought
Maybe he knew too

A snowy late winter day
Quietly slipping away
Yet unexpectedly finding him
Still tending to himself
Confessing he was too weak
My beloved carried him
Back to bed for the only time left
Darkness seeming to clap its hands

Night engulfed the low lit room
Please rest your agitation
I'll sit here with you—
Thinking he'd slip away in peace
Discovering otherwise so jarring
Combat ensuing in body and soul
Images that still run cold
Through my own disquieted veins

Hospice acquiesced to my request
He's struggling immensely—
Middle of the night comfort drugs
Arriving amid the snowstorm

To ease the death storm
He's battling and losing
This surely wasn't his choosing
Reaper perching atop his chest

Final words so cutting
My sister's face falls
How could he be so cruel
Aren't last words to be fuel
To sustain life hereafter
Providing comfort onward
Instead she steps away
Dealt this needless exchange

While mine a less criminal assault
Enduring restless bedside hours
Seeing her wounded heart
Breached the divide – ENOUGH –
My parental tone commands
For a brief moment he returns
Hearing the Dad I loved speak
Remorse and willing cooperation

While somewhat trained for this
Nothing prepares for this
The endless hours
The fleeting minutes
The slowing of breath
Leading to doorway of death
This night of darkest bother
Goodbye my dearest father

While relief holds hands with grief
Yet discomforting to admit
Faith builds a scaffold for hope
For any willing to climb it
I can still hear my dad singing
Blessed assurance Jesus is mine
For when all is done and all is said
Eternity bests the finite deathbed

02 March 24

LAST SUNDAY IN WARSAW

I sit here with a mixture
Of relief
And disbelief
To have watched a man's life
Go from repair
To despair
Or was it the other way around?

What was to be
Shall never be
And it was I
Who told him so
A heavy burden
Laid on me a second time
For I told the woman the same
Nearly seven years ago

Possessions reduced
To a concrete box
Locked tight
Without timeline
For reopening
They will lie in wait
Until a suitor beckons
Them into the light

I look ahead with caution
And slight taste of fear
For what lies ahead
Many unknowns,
Few givens except
For impending death
And when the bell tolls
We cannot know

I will return here
Fewer times ahead
Than behind
And will linger less
Take my steps to their grave
To pause with moist eyes
And then walk away

They are not here
Cold in the ground
But instead heavenly
Living more than
When alive

I look ahead
For that myself
Someday, yes, someday

12 March 2017

MAD

Watching TV
No clue this show
Has a string tied
To my heart
And with one tug
The tears begin to fall

Why didn't you
Face the truth?
Why did you
Have to stay
Stubborn
Choosing blinders?

I was there but
I don't know
If you died happy
Or if you went
Fighting all the way
To your last breath

I don't know
What you thought
Or felt really about me
In those last months
You were preoccupied
With your pipedream

I do know
That I'm mad
So angry
That you left
Without telling me
Anything

Things could've been
So different
But for some reason
You ignored what was real
Exchanging truth
For something else

And that something else
Has become my enemy
I've named it Denial
I hate it
I plan to dismantle it
One lie at a time

I know the end of the story
And it's good
God has not left me
Empty-handed
But instead
He holds mine

We only die once
And I promise
I will die
Differently
As God allows
Obedient to death

My kids will know
Without question
I deeply loved them
I truly liked them
I will not leave them
Mad

14 November 2017 - 8 months since you left us

TIMELESS

39 years ago today
you left me
my young heart was broken
there was no consoling
no amount of comfort
no help that could help

I could not understand
the 20 minute span
between you dying
and my delayed arriving
I was so unraveled by this
even now tears trail my cheek

how many times my asking why
was met with indifferent silence
God must be cruel –
yet I kept pleading
pounding on the gates of heaven
demanding an answer
still no words nor reply

I'd ask the same question
year upon saddened year
angry and brooding
or sullen and sad
no posture seemed to dignify
a response

it's been ten years
since I got my answer
and I've never forgotten
the cataclysmic shift
in my thinking and feeling
God isn't cruel afterall

to go from life to death
in an instant
would've been more
than my youth could handle
so God protected
whisking you home
before I arrived
to watch it with my own eyes

24 July 21

LUNCH

Grabbing a bite on my break
I hear someone I recognize
Right behind me
I know this voice—
But she died in September

The tears start to assemble
In my core and rise
Moments until they reach my eyes
Her intonations, her accent
Even her word choices
They are all hers

I'm strangely comforted
Simultaneously stricken
How can this be?
It must be her
Yet I don't dare look
I sit frozen, tears melting me

My meal is finished
I order coffee so I can linger
Selfishly sit a little bit longer
Just to hear her talk
To imagine she's still alive
In the booth at my back

The coffee cools
As I conjure a way
To bottle that voice
Open it another day
I miss her terribly—
What I'd give if I could

Isn't grief strange that way
The sum of us knows they're gone
But the stubborn part
Tugs at the possibility they aren't
Instead we want to play pretend
With someone sitting behind us at lunch

30 March 25

MOM

Thirteen plus years since
I put lotion on your feet
While you were dying—
Inhaled the bravest of breaths
Leaned in close
For a private moment with you
(I'm told hearing is the last to go)
So I told you everything
About your stroke
About the damage done
About your bleak prognosis
About how I was trusting you
And you were going to have to
Trust me too
That your signed wishes
One brief month prior
Were still your wishes now

Sis and Dad let me
Be the one to tell you
Because I'm the grief counselor
By training
Not
By daughter
Not
By prior experience
This was inexplicably hard
No one else
Could bear to tell you
So my breaking heart
Took a back seat
To truth steering the wheel
I knew you'd want that—
We had that kind of honesty
Between us

I've still not recovered
From those short, infinite
Minutes of time suspended
My words floating in the room
Terrified to land
And break your heart
You weren't going to make it—
I knew this would crush you
It was crushing me too
But I loved you enough
To painfully square with you
Mom, do you understand
What's happening

Until then you'd slept
All of three lifeless days
Except the few times
Your body would shift
Just a bit
Never opened your blue eyes
Never uttered a single word
Never again
Yet you were my mom one last time
By a sure and firm hand squeeze
Yours holding mine—
Somehow you heard
Somehow you knew
Somehow without word
Somehow I knew
Somehow now able
To let go of you

07 January 24

WHAT ABOUT YOUR TOYS?

It's getting close
Way too close
And I hate it
I'm so torn
My furry best friend
Are you in pain?
What is most humane?
And loving?

Oh there's been
SO
MUCH
LOVE
and my heart
Is breaking into
Pieces all over
My house

Your toys are strewn about
And greet me in every room
Even after I put them back
I find them everywhere
Because you drag them back out
Hoping for a game of tug

This is just like you too
You are everywhere –
I cannot walk an inch
Without signs of you
Meeting me
Greeting me
And soon
Leaving me

The tears have already
Started
Falling
And many sleeves
Will catch what falls
But what will catch
My heart?

It's a free fall
Into days ahead
Without you
I can barely see
Through the glaze
Of sadness
Flooding my eyes

You are a joy to me
You've been such a good boy to me
And what I'll have left
Will be memories
And your doggedly beloved toys
What will I do with these?

17 February 23

NUZZLE IN

You find me in low light
Starting my coffee
Head to the living room
For your first of many naps
You'll commandeer today

Once I'm settled
In my chair before dawn
You find me again
Enclosing the space
With your sweet fluffy face

Your aging doodle body
Wags from my nearness
You jut your snout
Into my free hand for pets
I lean into you

I breath you in
As I bury my nose
In your head's fluff
You indulge me
As I inhale you like air

Your turn—
My hair covers your nose
As you sniff and exhale
Our morning cuddles
Your low hmmms in my ear

I don't know how long
We'll get to do this
You hit your expiry date last month
But for as long as we have this
Nuzzle in, my sweet boy

23 May 24

WITH ME ALWAYS

I didn't expect grief
To be anything
But painful
 Obtrusive
  Inconvenient
   Gut wrenching
   Heart breaking
   Unwanted
Alarming
 Devastating
 Debilitating
  Engulfing
   Unexpected
    Oppressive
    Crushing
So absolutely cruel
I hate it

It made me so off-tilt
I couldn't right myself
By keeping hyperbusy
By faking okay
By hiding away
Life now and moving forward
At a permanent angle
As if gravity shifted
Forty-five degrees
Some days even more—
How will I walk like this
How will I stand
When all I want to do
Is join you in the ground
Curl beside you
And sleep forever

Greeted every morning
With this aching burden
Why can't this be a bad dream
How will I live out my days
Without you
The only constant is grief
With me always
Whether I laugh or cry
With me always
Whether sun or rain
With me always
No matter the day
With me always
As if it knows me

With me always
Becoming so familiar
That I resign it stay

So begin our walks together
A bond invisible and growing
While others come in and out
You don't leave me
I slowly begin to accept you
Inviting you to quietly settle
Into the best corner
Of my heart's home
It seems easier to share this place—
You already know my thoughts
You weather my ups and downs
Without a hint of judgement
Instead you hold my hand
So steady, so strong
Letting me be however I am
For however long I am
You comfort me
You accommodate me
I believe you truly get me
Unassumingly gentle
Ever present
I muse at my change of heart
Grief has become my friend

02 April 24

THEM

If he was the head
She was the heart
Both teaching me
Shaping me
Stretching me
A particular yet comforting
Cohesion developed in me
Through Mom and Dad

He gave me theology
The faith feet
To stand firm
The doctrine
To be discerning
Getting things sorted
For myself
Eventually also for others

She gave me psychology
The ability to befriend
To read people
The confidence
To start over as the new kid
To be brave and expectant
To understand myself
Eventually also others

They didn't always
Get it right
All too familiar shame
Permeated parenting
It was what they knew
How they had been raised
So they passed it on to me
Without mention

I went to therapy
Worked to undo some of it
Became a freer, lighter
Hopefully wiser version
I was made for this—
To deshame myself first
Eventually help others
Including dear them

They've been gone
For years now
I've held onto their good
I've said goodbye to the rest
I know they did their best
I'm working to do the same
It's all still love and gratitude
For them

13 July 24
Sealed with HML

FINAL DAYS

You've shown us all the signs
You've seemed at the end several times
Yet here you remain with us
While still slipping away from us

You've been the best boy
We've shared the best years
You've lovingly watched our boys
Grow into men with families
You've always been family too

One by one this week
We've said our goodbyes
In person, on FaceTime
Every time we leave the room
Alongside texts and well wishes
From so many who love you

Here I sit sad and stalled
Waiting for a dreaded house call
By a stranger who will help
I guess it's help
It doesn't feel like help

Go, run free, my beloved furry one
Let yourself rest in the arms of the One
Who created you, sent you to us
All the years you've seen us through
How we've loved every moment with you

Until it's time
I keep watch over your breaths
Your eyes open and close
To remind me you are fading
But oh how excruciating is the waiting

23 Sept 25

HEARTBROKEN

He's been gone two days
My heart is sufficiently broken
Turning into dust to dust
I'd take it back
If he wasn't failing so quickly
Weight falling dysmorphically
No matter what I tried to feed him
His legs without strength
His labored breathing without calm
His body trembling without chill
He was subsisting on laps of water
But that isn't sustainable

Bitter tears fall as I recall
His eyes peering into mine
Oh how I wanted him to tell me
What he wanted
What he really needed
How I could fix this for him
To not only prolong his life
But prevent his dying
Until I could go with him
Seriously
Until we could go together

Tuesday sadly wasn't a blur–
I watched him and the clock
I'd stop to check he was still breathing
I'd asked God to take him
Night after night
Laying at the foot of our bed
Knowing we had an appointment
A housecall I was dreading
The vet arrived
But dying was way ahead of her
Painfully happening inside me

Earlier I told him what was coming
I brought all his beloved toys to him
A huddle of his favorite friends
Last looks and innocent goodbyes
Did he know how loved he was
Could he feel it now
Alongside the sedative
We held him close
So his last thing he'd hear was us
Go to sleep baby
We love you
You are the best boy

We love you
Let your body rest now
We love you
Shhhh sweet boy
We love you Oakley

So trusting even while so weak
He slipped into the quiet
Heart still beating
We stroked his silky hair over and over
To soothe him and us
But nothing soothes this kind of loss
Fifteen minutes like this
Then the final stop of life itself
I hate everything about this
I hate it so much I can barely breathe
Then the complete and utter still
His body motionless
For the first time in his life
Here now was death

Lifted into grieving arms
His body lithe as if a puppy again
Scooped up when into mischief
Now being carried up the hill
It took me back thirteen years
How unexpectedly comforting
This image that had been forgotten
Until I watched the final steps

Wrapped in a soft white blanket
With his best toy friend Freddie
We laid him to rest in the cherry grove
It's peaceful in their midst
You can see everything from there
The deer come in from the forest
The turkeys file into the upper yard
To poke at the soft grasses
I'll place a writing table there
So I can be near him
Until I can join him

I'm left with tear soaked memories
Thoughts and images that intrude
I want only to hear his collar tags
His nails clicking across wood floors
His approach for kisses and hugs
I held him every chance I got
Wrapping my arm underneath him
To steady him and whisper to him
You're my good good boy
 I love you so much, so so much

The place he secretly rests
Marks for us something final
My husband visits often each day
But I cannot venture there yet
All in good time it will come
Through the changing seasons
Laughter and memories will return
Ever so slow the path to healing
Day by day it settles inside me
The reality he is truly gone
I look to the little dog left behind
His deep gaze and abiding nearness
His own lostness like ours
As I ask him this vexing question
What are we going to do
Without Oakley

25 Sept 25

CHAPTER 8:

I was born and lived in Ohio to age three and returned seven years later after living in West Virginia, Alabama, and Oregon in between. We headed to Indiana for junior and senior high school before I left for college in Illinois, then back to Indiana, then to the Chicago suburbs while I was in seminary. Marriage moved me to Florida for one and a half years until we made our way back to the Chicago area for the next 30. The only thing I would ever consider reason enough to leave my Midwest would be my kids and their families. So—we moved to New York in July of 2024, one day after our first grandchild was born in NYC. This move was the twentieth for me and I hope any future moves are in the single digits.

The Midwest is in my blood. I know its seasonal colors and landscapes, its flora and fauna, its mid-winter ice storms, fall festivals, summer sunsets and goodhearted people. I still get particularly homesick for Chicago, the beloved place I've spent more than half my life in both its suburbs and city proper. While I now live in New York's Hudson Valley and my home overlooks the great river, my heart almost aches at times for the varying blues of Lake Michigan. I miss the way its water sloshes back and forth as if a giant bathtub on a windy day on Lake Shore Drive, how it lays still most days before sunrise, and entreats my soul to breathe deeply when I take in its aqua hues.

My history is woven into the fibers of the Midwest, the deepest roots this transplant has ever grown, and the dearest friends of my life are all there. I purposefully invested in deep and abiding relationships with so many beautiful people over the decades there, the kind that I can pick up with as if I saw them hours ago. These dearly beloved are some of my life's most treasured gifts—I thank God for each of them, many of whom have lovingly shared in and cheered on my process of writing this book.

Since moving to New York, I've had numerous people tell me they've never been to Chicago so I wax poetically if they'll indulge me, to entice them to visit and validate my love for it. I believe at this point in my life the Midwest will always feel like my home and I'm glad for it. But deeper still is my true home on this side of eternity—wherever my husband and sons and their families are living out this wondrous life. Goodbye my Midwest, I loved you well.

MY MIDWEST

I loved the region, my Midwest
Its familiar beloved four seasons
Miles of open sky and sunsets
A mix of interstates and gravel roads
Creeks, ponds, and lakes
Subtle drawls in speech

Summer showcased county fairs
Pristine soybean and corn fields
Backyards alight with fireflies
Barbecued everything
Every small town boasting
Theirs the best ice cream stand

Fall ushered in harvest festivals
Pumpkin farms with hayrides
Piles of raked leaves to jump in
Pre-holiday craft bazaars
Cooks readying their kitchens
For all things holiday

Winters were often brutally cold
Dreadfully elongated
Zoos dressed in holiday lights
Neighborhood cookie exchanges
Church Christmas pageants
All marking advent season
Before the dreary gray set in

Spring breathed bleak landscapes
Back to life with verdant green
Flowering trees lined main streets
Thunderstorms watered grass
As the hum of lawnmowers returned
People shedding hibernation to play

Half of my life collected here
I've assuredly aggrandized it
It wasn't all sunsets and sweet corn
My family might even laugh at this
But for this New York transplant
I miss it still, my Midwest.

04 August 25

LAST THINGS

They closed it today —
Buckingham Fountain
The cascading hoses
Of three firetrucks
Empty thousands of its gallons
Into the beloved Lake Michigan
A long six months ahead
Winter is coming
I pause and take it in
So much will happen in six months
My cherished friends have no idea
But something else is coming
I catch my breath and hold it
As my car inches up the Drive
I peer inland into the city
To see white twinkle lights
Leading towards the Mag Mile
Christmas is coming
The announcing parade
Is two weeks away
My gaze is drawn again to the shore
The lake so strangely calm
The gray of autumn's sky
Washes into the gray of the water
Indecipherable horizon at dusk
Bikers in jackets and
Joggers on the path
Know the bitter chill that's coming
Some of the last things
Are coming into view for me
As I make my way home
I won't be here
This time next year
Instead, I'll be learning
A new state
A new city
A new neighborhood
A new house
A new address
You can't have first things
Without having last things
It feels neutral now
But before long it won't
Memorize the things I love
Less agonizing goodbyes
To the things I don't
My mind records these last things
Soon enough they'll be past things

TRADING

I'm trading high ceilings
For the vast sky above
The open floor plan
For property and a yard to love
Everything on one floor
To many levels of delight

I'm trading light pollution
For star gazing when I choose
Building obstructions
For stunning sunset views
Unseeable celestial events
For falling stars I can watch

I'm trading houseplants
For lovely landscaping
A fake fiddle leaf fig
For trees that flower
Rugs that we vacuum
For grass that we mow

I'm trading city noises
For birds singing
Sirens and delivery trucks
For the morning dove's song
The lake's summer breezes
For the river valley view

I'm trading two flights of stairs
For the climb in our backyard
The gas grill on the balcony
For an outdoor fire circle
Pots of herbs and small tomatoes
For a garden we can grow

I'm trading my dog on a leash
For the yard he can explore
The mice in our pantry
For foxes and wild turkeys
The rats in the alley
For deer feeding at dusk

I'm trading landlord renting
For owning acreage all ours
A tight Houdini garage
For a three-car and driveway
A foyer mail slot
For a flagged mailbox on a post

I'm trading my beloved big city
For a new small enclave
Public transit and Uber
For wandering new sidewalks
Takeout and delivery
For becoming a regular in town

Doesn't really seem fair
But I am indeed gladly
Trading

27 April 24

KNOWN

To be known and loved
Is the greatest thing life gives
So much more than
My name, my profession, etc.
Those barely qualify really

I'm leaving the Midwest to move east
Farther east than I've ever lived
And I don't know a soul
Scarier yet, not a soul knows me
To be honest
This is so unsettling

Florida was never my home—
The short stint when newly married
I was glad to leave its sand two years in
Return to my four season roots
Plant my life in good soil and grow
A family, yet more decidedly, myself

Now I'm uprooting by choice
Yet in part it's choosing me
Our family is adding one
Life on life draws me to move
Without her being born yet
What a powerful little magnet
She is becoming

I've started again nineteen times
New York will make it twenty
It's still just as hard
Even though I now know myself well
Is there enough time ahead
Will they know me, ever get to
Like I am now, known

22 April 24
Sealed with PIC

LAST DAY

Boxes everywhere
Chaos more accurately
Coffee is priority
In my first waking moments
The grinder obeys
The kettle obliges
The predawn dark lingers

I settle into my chair
Warm Christmas mug in hand
From my partner in crime
Inhale the air of the cup
Before I sip its dark gold
Two forms of comfort
Essential
To begin this last day

A 9-pin awaits me—
My reference in this career
For clients on my schedule
It's been a series of tears
Goodbyes spanning years
All the intimate pains
The deep desires for change
Healing bit by bit
I will miss this
I miss it already

The virtual world cannot
Fulfill being face to face
Doesn't come close
To being in the room
Still the time has come
I'm moving to the northeast—
So my beloved Midwest census
Transitions to sessions
At what feels a great distance
Yet we will do this

I feel it deeply
My heart aches
To close this chapter
Open a new one
For many good reasons
But it still hurts
To say goodbye
Client after client
I'll still see them next week
Just through a tiny camera

So my coffee grows cold
As I wave off the day
The ceiling fan quietly whirs
City life begins to stir
The clock moves forward
No matter how much I want
To procrastinate today
Be brave, girl—
You will face this some way
You can do this last day

30 May 24

SLOWING

Finding myself lately
Tucking moments away
How your eyes actually sparkle
As you smile at me
A puppy's chin that rests
On my shoulder like a baby
Intertwined notes that play
Reeling my heart in closer
The sun kisses my cheek
Warm breezes waft by
I'm disengaging from frenzy
Just for these kinds of things

When I'm distracted
I miss absolutely
All of this and more
But when I pause
Oh my God when I pause
It's deep, tender, lifelike
The storehouse of good
Comes tumbling out
My heart swells in joy
Don't ever-loving lose this

Please just drop me off
So I can catch my breath
Suspend all that's needless
Stop this noisy world
Everyone please just stop—
Take some deep inhales
Close your tired eyes
Isn't this so good??
I promise you
Busy is a liar and a thief

Let the moment here sit
Feet dangling
From a happy stool
I'm small once again
All is well with my world
Not a single care
No more burgling fears
It's quite perfect
Just sitting here
Near tears

02 June 24
Sealed with JF

EMPTY THIS PLACE

Six years lived here
Nearly to the day
A most lovely abode
A place we've enjoyed
And loved so well

Boxes are stacked
Halfway up the walls
Every room a mess
All strong signs
We are leaving

Empty this place—
Load our home
Onto the rental truck
Fill it full with life
Close its sliding door

Let this return
To being just a city flat
It's been so mixed
With the madness
Of a contentious owner

Yet I've loved living here
Memories so rich
The parties, the holidays
The laughter
Light ruins darkness

I'll recall all its good
Discard all the sour
Wrap it up in a box
Fit for safe travel
Time to empty this place

25 June 24
Sealed with PIC

THREE LITTLE BOYS

Three little boys on Howland Avenue
Motioning me to honk my horn
They jump with glee when I do
This never happened in Chicago
I'm in a new small New York enclave
Where hydrangea bushes are blue

The next town over on Main Street
Four people with seeing-eye dogs
Are being trained to cross the street
People patiently wait
Smiles are exchanged
No indignant horns blaring
From commuters late to work

I have this swell of hope inside
I'm going to be okay
There are good people here—
It's been over forty years
Since I lived in a small town
Dust off my how are you's
Shake out my good mornings
Settle in to recognizing faces
As I make new friends

How does a Chicago girl
Find her way here
One exchange at a time
Take the time to converse
Get to know them
Remember their names
Remind them of mine
It will all be fine

Maybe, just maybe
I'll start to feel at home here
I'll make my way into town
Without my gps
Greet the coffee baristas
By name with a smile
Notice the commotion outside
Running down the sidewalk
Here come those three little boys

07 July 24

CHAPTER 9:

It's strange to get to this final chapter not knowing how many more chapters in my life are yet to be written. What I do know is that time is fleeting and making the most of our days is crucial. While most days are ordinary and uneventful, not packed with intentionally curated moments, finding meaning in each day is a valuable mindset. I look back over my life and find myself smiling, recalling laughter with loved ones, green-tailed shooting stars, thousands of amazing meals, family game tournaments, sleeping babies, tender hugs, and great cups of coffee. I've had the blessing of travel, soaking in many breathtaking places, alongside walking in some of the darkest places of the soul with myself and others. To me, the sum of life is sacred and makes being human a wildly packaged gift. It's ours to unwrap it and see what's inside.

I've chosen these last few poems as a way to share glimpses of what it's like to put my arm around my younger self and let her know I see her, I know her very well, and I like her. I remember her being hurt and how it mattered, I've understood her guarded curiosity decades after her first heartbreak, I've encouraged her wonderment in being able to heal, and I've appreciated her hard emotional work she's poured into these poems. There's something powerful that happens when you allow yourself to integrate all the pieces of self with its gamut of feelings, thoughts, behaviors, and experiences that make up your life. It's been deeply rewarding to make peace with my past, make sense of the things I couldn't control and find value in the choices I made to bring me to today. This process reflects my way of bringing my life out into the light and how in doing so has allowed me to find Joy.

JOY

My name was a curse
Most of my life
A little girl
Not allowed
To be sour or foul
Because she wasn't
Living up to her name

What a terrible thing
To lay on a tiny heart
Shaming the negative
Praising the positive
Life isn't
That black and white
To a forming soul

I didn't want
Christmas ornaments
Bearing my moniker
When the other kids
Got Legos or paint kits
At the party
Gift exchange

I was a funny happy girl
Who also had justice
In her veins
So not all was light
Able to buoy up
The adults in my house
For happy's sake

The just part of me
Began to resent
The name and its weight
Let me feel my feelings
All of them
Without shame
Like my sister gets to

I had it out with God at 50—
Why this name?
It's been a lifelong burden
I hear somewhere inside
Your name is Joy
Because that's how I feel
About you

In that instant
Something broke
Something healed
No longer in chains
I can now embrace the depth
I can finally be and feel
Joy

07 January 24

YOUNGER SELF

You couldn't have known
When you were three
You'd grow out of
Being afraid of sirens
Being so short
You couldn't reach
The door handle
To get inside
When the noon bell sounded
But you sure did try

You couldn't have known
You'd move eleven times
By seventh grade
Making temporary friends
Never a lifelong one—
Until you were decades old
Making the mistake
Of telling you were moving
Finding yourself alone
On the playground too soon

You couldn't have known
Your first true love
Wasn't
You would go through
Many iterations
Before forever came along
Even then it would take work
Nearly falling apart
Before you figured it out
For keeps

You couldn't have known
The college friends
Who you loved dearly
Would end up
In your rear view mirror
In a few short years
A series of memories
That righted you
Into adulthood
They were just a season

You couldn't have known
Changing your major
Would result
In the most wonderful path
To a career you love

Helping amazing people
Broken but so beautiful
Open to receive care
Teaching you far more
Than you've imparted to them

Time has taught you
All things age beyond maturity
Entropy is inevitable
Growth is optional
Joy is essential
To live well
To end well
Wonderful you now know
What you couldn't have then

10 March 24

IT'S BEST I LEAVE US

Not sure why lately
You've been dancing
Through my mind
Laughing playfully
Trampling the path
Of my wildflower heart
Pausing to recollect
Something special
We once had

I see you still
In memory's portico
You're so young
So perfect
So alive with love
I can hardly take it
My heart actually hurts
I need to look away
I need to leave this here

Hopefully unnoticed
I found you yesterday
No profile pictures
But certain it's you,
Your hometown too
And my heart skipped
An unsettling beat
This is definitely you
This is definitely yours

Have you thought of me
Over decades of years
Does your mind trail back
To those collection of days
When all was well
With the world of us
We were young
We were alive
We felt infinite
But we weren't

I allow my heart
One more glance
Test it and see
If tears won't form
When I intently look

Into memory's gaze
Your eyes locked on mine
This isn't a good idea
It's best I leave us
Where you left me

18 May 24

TIME

The good book says
There's a time for everything
I've seen it
I breathe it
I believe it

While minutes can drag
Years fly by
It's a new day
A new year
Wasn't it just Y2K?

My baby
Is having a baby
Those who gave me life
Are long gone
The circle loops on

My brown locks
Mix with silver now
My brown eyes
Need help to see
Yet I'm still fully me

Time is a frenemy
Sometimes in my favor
Other times against me
But always moving
Oh to be time free
Someday in eternity

19 January 24
Sealed with HS

APRIL 24

I finished a book yesterday
Listening with eyes closed
Over two days of hours
No warning what was coming
Breaking archaea open
Deep, deep inside me
Forty-four years buried
I thought it was healed
I thought it was gone

The audiobook's actor
Somehow accessed
The saddest most ruined place
Of my young girl heart
I didn't know why I was crying
But I was certainly crying
As something leagues deep
Exploded to the surface
In a fast sickening ascent
Revealing it was always there
Uncharted until yesterday

Today I'm still stunned
Hearing the voice in my head
Unable to replay it out loud
Afraid it could break me further
That debilitating disbelief
Of love burning down
Fiercely refusing its end
Stirring from emotion's trench
The most wrenching loss
The most empty place
I've ever miserably known

This drilled down sadness
Has gripped me
So unexpectedly
Collapsing my heart
Did I not reach the bottom
Decades ago
Only to discover now
There was no floor
It's a free fall once again
Dear God please no—
Catch me from descending
I barely survived it at sixteen

Somehow I'll find repair
I've been through this before—
Never planned its return
Resurfacing unawares
Shaken, yes
Saddened, indeed
Ruined, not a chance
My heart's walls rattled
Comfort arrives carefully
Resetting all back in place
Healing takes such a long time

13 March 24

THERAPOETIC

I've engaged a new therapist
After years going without
Three prior painful seasons
Putting myself on the couch
Starting over each time
At a completely new place
In the journey of living
Moving toward dying
Perhaps a bit more intact
Than if I had chosen not

This time it's more expansive
Touching its depth and breadth
With golden hands and open heart
I'm far more brave
Than in years past
My bifocal eyesight
Seeing so much clearer
Crystalline realizations
Bursting on the scene
What delight to be seen

I'm not sure her origin
But her training proves
Helpful and heartfelt
Asking provoking questions
She allows to sit in the air
Until they settle inside me
And waits—
Waits for uninhibited answers
To emerge
So patient, so tender
So benevolent for my soul

She grants me long pauses
Sometimes for days
To weigh and lift upwards
My sadness from the years
Of holding others' grief
The counterbalance to burden
Just so that they could be free
Even if for a moment
Until their feet return under them
Something that sometimes takes
Unmeasurable amounts of time

She's invited me to this process
I've gladly embraced
Looking out over my life
With its edgeless perimeter
Someday whose borders
Will be noted and locked
But for now unending
Exploring the wild places
My instrumental confidant
This surprising therapeutic pen

13 March 24

FISTS

If your words were fists
I would've healed
Much sooner

They take me back
To younger days
Barely three, innocent

Big brother rage
Scared the pee
Out of me

No idea
What I'd done
For this

Wrath and anger
Preyed upon me
Left alone to cry

And now I'm older
You can't harm me
Anymore

Or so I thought
Until your words
Slapped me

The sting returned
Searing memories
Hot with tears

Now I guard her
I'm her keeper
I comfort her

You haven't changed
But I have
I've done my work

So I walk free
But you are still
In chains

31 August 21

PEN AND INK

I'd sign my name
To these thoughts
Revised and rewritten
Long enough
Making it legit

If you asked me
The truth
I'd push this paper
Across the table
For you to read

No more hedging
Or negotiating
You need to see this
Whether you accept this
It's still true

You are mean
And bitter
And your words
Are ugly
They do great harm

I reject your hate
I repel your lies
I rebuke your labels
I resist revenge
I walk away instead

Silent distance helps
And heals the wounds
I'm staying away
For good reason
Leave me alone

The ink has dried
The page has yellowed
But the truth remains
I am stronger now
And in ways softer

Your hurt
Came from somewhere
But it's not mine
To carry or soothe
Here is a pen

31 August 21

CRYING

Why am I crying
Listening to a song
I've never heard before
Whose unexpected words
Drill into my tunneled heart

I kept my head down
Crossing lonely months
Pushing to achieve
My big dream—
Up and running now

Jump my sleeping soul
With meted melodic sparks
Chords of deep bass
Prose without rhyme
Restart my parched life

Neglected life on blocks
Had no need for fuel
Just get through this—
Think, don't feel for now
You'll be alright

I hear tear-stained words
Commending, upending
What was all but gone
Bringing life back
To my rusting frame

It's good to finally look up
Taking in this song
That rends my waking heart
Don't forget this reminder—
The best is yet to come

Inspired by Judah & The Lion, The Best is Yet to Come

IS THIS WHAT IT'S LIKE?

Not every thought
Becomes a line in a poem
Some things
Are better left unsaid—
There's this verse
In the good book:
"The heart knows its own bitterness
No stranger shares its joy"
So I'm content
To leave some things
There, unwritten
Quiet in my soul

But at other times
I cordon myself off
Alone with my thoughts
Social calendar lighter
Longer spans of stillness
Just to think
Pause
Observe
Reflect
Reworking ideas
Into lines fit for the page
Yet maybe they still aren't —
There's room for that too

Is this what it's like
To be a writer?
Stretched spans of time
Seasons of rhyme
A frenzy of words vying
To step single file out of my head
Becoming the lines
That will someday be read
I really don't mind it
After talking for 30 years—
This is nice for a change
Inviting myself pause
With a cup of coffee
To see what comes out
On the paper
Like this

02 January 24

REWARD

If I lack sufficient talent
According to the world's standards
It's still absolutely worth it
To enjoy what I've done
To laugh at myself
To put my arm around my ego
Give it a squeeze and a smile
And say I like you
I really truly like you

I've said for years
I don't care much what others think
And for the most part, I mean it
Who gets to set the standard?
Who decides what is good?
Or better still, what is talent?
Is it just a popularity vote
Amassing virtual likes?
Or is it something deeper
That results
Like intrinsic, personal delight?

I choose to make my life matter
To think on some level
I've made a difference
Even if just for one soul —
That feels satisfying
Not needing another's approval
To assign or dictate value
Based on their skewed opinion
Or personal preferences

I've been listening to Thoreau
More than a century post mortem
Not as impressive as touted
Once I learned his backstory
The same is just as true of me—
Yet I'm still glad to tuck away
For safekeeping
Some thoughts to ponder
Long after I've left this earth
Maybe they will give birth
To another writer's wonderings

How splendid the thought
Maybe the aforementioned poet
Accomplished his goal after all
By making his home in the woods

To take in the whole of nature
Pontificate his observations
In excess, in my opinion

While I won't move away
From my loved ones like he did
I've cordoned off space and time
To observe, ponder, and create
In retrospect the process is similar
We have to walk a distance
From the routine of life
To let the words find paper
To me it's truly worth the work

October 2024

WAITING

Waiting until I have enough
But honestly
Will it ever be enough
The mass of words
That are frequent flyers
In my brain
Land less often
Than I'd like

I'm genius
When I'm driving
Or falling asleep
And the words
Roll out of me
Like artesian springs
But when I have a pen
I'm simple and slow

I could do this forever
With nothing to show
And that would be cruel
For all the years
I've composed
And written
My soul out
On paper

Take the leap, girl
Find your way
Push your heart out
In front of you
Be the model
For braving critics
Loving those words more
Than fearing flame throwers

Waiting turns
To walking out
Steps on purpose
And the nod of heads
Leads to signatures
And the presses roll
Hand me the book
Waiting is over

18 September 23

REFLECTION

These poems are honest
Not all happy sing-song rhymes
But honest—
Sometimes comedic
Sometimes pained
Like bare feet on craggy rocks
Other times they have rolled
Out of me like melted butter
Spreading a thin shiny layer of gold
Over my memories
I'm glad for all of it—
The hard things
The not so pretty things
The things others might wish
I'd never written
The special things
Enveloped magical moments
Glittered with people I love
And how I have loved them all
The amazing places I can still see
In my photographic memory
Every bit of my senses
Having been revisited
As if just moments ago
And finally, so happily penned
It's good
It's all very, very good
And I am beyond thankful
To have lived thus far
And for who knows
How much longer
I've made my life
A reflecting pool
I see myself better now
Please do this as well—
Live on my friend,
Thrive and live well
Figure out your eternity
While you remain
So those who love you
Can someday say goodbye
And ultimately grieve well
When you too become
Just a reflection

09 December 23

SCARED

I've told my clients for years
There's no need for courage unless you're scared–

My twilight thoughts rouse me to rise uncomfortably early
The nearly full moon is soon to set over the Hudson Valley horizon
Reminding darkness that it will not triumph
The thick pitch-black of my living room
Is pressed away by lighting the fire
Why couldn't the criminal trespass of intrusive thoughts
Wait until morning
Instead of robbing me of slumber

I've somehow managed to finish my memoir
It's resulting weightiness
Presses my brain to wake up
Rife with anxiety
Begging more questions than answers
For writing a book is no small task
Even if deeply rewarding–

I've used the word "fun" too many times
To describe this process
Conveying ease with innocent confidence
But in this moment feeling shortsighted and foolish
I don't know what I don't know
The bulk of this endeavor remains foreign to me
This is uncomfortably daunting

It was just a hobby in simpler days
Now embodying something bigger than myself
Like a journey far greater than its arrival point
I was a little girl born into a particular family
No sights on becoming a therapist
My eight year old self dreamed of being a florist
Yet life took its turns into people and places and experiences
Farther afield than a field of flowers
Therapy called me
Therapy shaped me
Therapy helped me
More than I've helped others

The edited manuscript is now with my designer
I'm on the precipice of this becoming a physical book
I   am   scared   –
Everyone cheers in the bleachers of support
But I am the one required to take the next trepidatious steps
I could let this remain a private passion project
Sell a few dozen copies to my bevy of friends
Leave it at that

Why must these nagging thoughts
Forcibly push me into the literary room of exposure
All eyes are on me
This is so much more than a case of cold feet
Tripping on aged floors

So now, beloved self, career therapist,
Embrace your own frequented words
With a tight, reassuring hug
There's no need for courage unless you're scared
You can do this
You must do this
These risks make you stronger on all emerging levels of self
Yet strange is the path of penned poems
Becoming the enduring record of my life

30 January 26
Sealed with MA

TONIGHT

I didn't think tonight was possible
Gathering my treasured people
The ones who make up my life
Each wonderful one of you
To help me pause
Catch my breath
Before I step into my 6th decade

I was going to allow life
And it's demands to dictate
And overshadow the important
Until one early morning twilight
I knew I couldn't miss this—
One last party here
One final chance
To have you all in the same room

I could write endless poems
They wouldn't ever be enough—
To pen your unmeasurable value
To find the words that say
How much I love you
How much I need you
How wowed I am by God
That he brought you into my life

This is just a small attempt
To make sure you know
You are the ones I hold dearest
While you matter to so many others
I somehow get to know you too
Share life with you
Watch you grow
Watch you be you

I hope you take from tonight
That celebrating is essential
Loving on purpose matters
Clasping hands while we can
Because one by one
We will each step from earth
Into our promised eternity

I know it will be a long time
Before we all gather again, there
So look around this room

Soak in the beauty
Of our collective worth
Be assured you have given me
The most wonderful gift I call tonight

04 May 24
Sealed with my tribe at my 60th Birthday Party

Let them easily forget who I am, let them instead recall what was said.
–Joy

www.ingramcontent.com/pod-product-compliance
Lightning Source LLC
Chambersburg PA
CBHW081359130726

47998CB00011B/3017